MW00573972

Music Fundamentals for Musical Theatre

Online resources to accompany this book are available at:
https://www.musicfundamentalsformusicaltheatre.com

Music Fundamentals for Musical Theatre

Christine Riley

methuen | drama

LONDON · NEW YORK · OXFORD · NEW DELHI · SYDNEY

METHUEN DRAMA
Bloomsbury Publishing Plc
50 Bedford Square, London, WC1B 3DP, UK
1385 Broadway, New York, NY 10018, USA

BLOOMSBURY, METHUEN DRAMA and the Methuen Drama logo are trademarks of Bloomsbury Publishing Plc

First published in Great Britain 2020

Copyright © Christine Riley, 2020

Christine Riley has asserted her right under the Copyright, Designs and Patents Act, 1988,
to be identified as author of this work.

For legal purposes the Permissions Acknowledgments on pp. 271–9 constitute an extension of this copyright page.

Cover image © Lisa Kolbasa / Shutterstock

All rights reserved. No part of this publication may be reproduced or transmitted in any form or by any means, electronic
or mechanical, including photocopying, recording, or any information storage or retrieval system, without prior permission
in writing from the publishers.

Bloomsbury Publishing Plc does not have any control over, or responsibility for, any third-party websites
referred to or in this book. All internet addresses given in this book were correct at the time of going to press.
The author and publisher regret any inconvenience caused if addresses have changed or sites have ceased to exist,
but can accept no responsibility for any such changes.

A catalogue record for this book is available from the British Library.

Library of Congress Cataloging-in-Publication Data
Names: Riley, Christine (Music director) author.
Title: Music fundamentals for musical theatre / Christine Riley.
Description: [1.] | New York : Bloomsbury Publishing Plc, 2020. | Includes bibliographical references and index. | Summary:
"Musical theatre students and performers are frequently asked to learn musical material in a short space of time; sight-read
pieces in auditions; collaborate with accompanists; and communicate musically with peers, directors, music directors and
choreographers. Many of these students and performers will have had no formal musical training. This book offers a series of
lessons in music fundamentals, including theory, sight-singing and aural tests, giving readers the necessary skills to navigate
music and all that is demanded of them, without having had a formal music training. It focuses on the skills required of the
musical theatre performer and draws on musical theatre repertoire in order to connect theory with practice. Throughout the
book, each musical concept is laid out clearly and simply with helpful hints and reminders. The author takes the reader back to
basics to ensure full understanding of each area. As the concepts begin to build on one another, the format and process is kept
the same so that readers can see how different aspects interrelate. Through introducing theoretical ideas and putting each
systematically into practice with sight-singing and ear-training, the students gain a much deeper and more integrated
understanding of the material, and are able to retain it, using it in voice lessons, performance classes and their professional lives.
Music Fundamentals for Musical Theatre allows aspirational performers - and even those who aren't enrolled on a course - to
access the key components of music training that will be essential to their careers"— Provided by publisher.
Identifiers: LCCN 2019043970 | ISBN 9781350001756 (paperback) | ISBN 9781350001794 (hardback) | ISBN 9781350001763
(pdf) | ISBN 9781350001770 (epub) | ISBN 9781350001787
Subjects: LCSH: Musical theater–Instruction and study. | Music theory.
Classification: LCC MT956 .R58 2020 | DDC 782.1/4142—dc23
LC record available at https://lccn.loc.gov/2019043970.

ISBN: HB: 978-1-3500-0179-4
         PB: 978-1-3500-0175-6
         ePDF: 978-1-3500-0176-3
         eBook: 978-1-3500-0177-0

Typeset by RefineCatch Limited, Bungay, Suffolk

To find out more about our authors and books visit www.bloomsbury.com
and sign up for our newsletters.

CONTENTS

Introduction: Why Music Fundamentals for Musical Theatre Students?

When I was first asked to teach a college course for musical theatre students that incorporated music theory and sight-singing, I began searching for an appropriate textbook. I did not find a book or series of books that covered what I thought was necessary and instead began creating worksheets for my students. The worksheets and assignments eventually developed into the text you see today. As a musical theatre performer, you need to be able to read music and communicate effectively with pianists, coaches and music directors. Actors are often required to learn large amounts of music in a short period of time, whether it is a call-back packet containing four songs to learn in twenty-four hours or a twenty-nine-hour reading of a new show. In both scenarios, you not only need to learn the music, but are also expected to make character choices based on the material in front of you. Learning to analyze a piece of music quickly is an invaluable tool for a musical theatre performer. Many music theory books and courses focus on classical music. In most music schools, music majors take four to eight semesters of music theory and sight-singing classes. They have time to delve into Handel, Puccini, and Tchaikovsky. While this is a necessary skill for students that are performing this material, it is a luxury that many musical theatre performers do not have. Actors, whether studying in a conservatory, university, or on their own, have to devote an equal amount of time to training as an actor, dancer, and singer. Therefore, I have chosen to focus the book on the basics of what you will encounter and use on a daily basis. Whether you are learning the material on your own or as part of a class, you should be able to hone your musical skills and walk in to any audition or rehearsal situation with confidence.

How/What Will You Learn?

The book covers rhythm, major and minor keys, intervals, triads, seventh chords, phrasing, sight-singing, dictation, and song analysis. All of the musical excerpts come from the musical theatre repertoire spanning George Gershwin to Jason Robert Brown. The first nine chapters of the book focus solely on learning to hear and perform basic rhythms and intervals. I use moveable "do" solfege for sight-singing. I find that it is the easiest way for you to incorporate the theoretical knowledge of intervals into performance. The syllables are comfortable to sing and are easily adjustable for minor keys and accidentals. If you, the student or teacher, prefer a different method, it is possible to perform all of the examples in any format. As a singer, it can be difficult to "see" and hear a melodic or harmonic line. I use the piano keyboard to give you a visual representation of each interval as well as musical theatre song examples to offer an aural representation of each interval. The constant reference to the piano keyboard also (without discussing piano technique) creates a familiarity with the piano, giving you the ability to "plunk" out parts and basic chords if necessary. As each chapter progresses, new intervals and rhythms are added to the sight-singing exercises. The website provides examples in each chapter to give you a guide to work with while learning. There are also suggested songs to work on and listen to from the musical theatre repertoire.

In Chapter 10, triads are introduced. As we work through identifying and writing triads, chord progressions, and inversions, there are numerous song examples to look at and listen to as well as choral sight-singing examples. If you are in a classroom setting, you can sing through the choral examples as a group to hear how the individual parts fit together. If you are working as an individual, you can sing through each part, analyze the chords, and listen to a recording. Although the theory focus shifts to chords and harmony, there are still plenty of melodic sight-singing examples to work on. The examples get progressively harder and incorporate new rhythmic concepts every few chapters.

As you work through each chapter, you will see sections titled SONG ANALYSIS. Each of these sections combines the skills you are learning with insight into using those skills to analyze the music. You will learn to interpret different aspects of the music for clues to character development and emotional arc. Each new song analysis section gives you new tools to dig deeper into the "how" and "why" of the music. The song analysis sections culminate in Chapter 24, where you use all of the tools you have learned to analyze larger and more complicated musical examples.

In addition, at the end of each review chapter, you will find performance tips to help you navigate and understand your sheet music more fully. Although they are located in the review chapters, they each contain very important new information that you don't want to miss!

How Does All of This Knowledge Help Me as a Performer?

This may seem obvious, but knowing how to read music gives you the ability to **learn your music** on your own. As a performer you will be given a considerable amount of music to learn over your education and career. Ideally you don't want to have to rely on someone else to teach you every note; it is expensive! Your time with a coach is better served shaping and crafting your piece, not learning the notes. When you can read music, you have the tools to:

- clap and count through the rhythms;
- speak your lyrics in rhythm;
- learn the melody (or harmony) using solfege;
- play the melody or chords on the piano;
- interpret musical markings.

Next, you will be a more confident performer in your **auditions** if you can read music. Auditions are often a stressful process, but if you are confident in your music, your cut, talking to the pianist, and learning callback materials, you will be taking away many of the factors that are often a worry to performers. Using your music theory knowledge you are able to:

- create a 16-, 8-, or 32-bar cut;
- check to see if you are singing a complete phrase;
- look at the chords to see if your cut resolves or ends on tonic;
- talk to the pianist about tempo;
- talk to the pianist about any special markings;
- learn music quickly for a callback (possibly even out in the hallway while waiting to be seen again)!

Finally, when you are **cast in a show**, you often have a lot of material to learn (possibly in a short period of time). It is always best to come into music rehearsals with your melodies learned so that the music director can work with you on shaping the music instead of playing out your part. You also have the benefit of being able to:

- learn your harmony lines faster;
- be flexible when changes are made to the music;
- understand rhythm and counts to help with dance steps;
- analyze your music to gain a deeper understanding of your character's emotional state and conflict and resolution points.

As you work through the book, take your time. Some chapters may take a few days to master, while others may take weeks. Use the website (https://www.musicfundamentalsformusicaltheatre.com) to listen to examples of the material and to work on listening and dictation. Although you may not ever need to transcribe (write what you hear) in your career, it is a tremendous help to train your ears and become a stronger musician.

Practice sight-singing every day. Use the examples in the book, but also use material you are working on for a voice lesson or an audition. Learning to sight-sing takes time. The best way to train your ears and your voice is with consistent practice. Don't be afraid to work on very short sections at a time. If necessary, sing one measure and then check your starting pitch and your final pitch with the piano. Record yourself doing each exercise and then play it back to find your mistakes. If you are having trouble with a particular interval, try singing up or down the scale to find the note and then jump back and forth between the two pitches until you are comfortable. Work on the more difficult parts and re-record. Finally, use a metronome while working on rhythm and sight-singing—it will help you feel the division of the beat within a steady tempo.

In my experience, musical theatre performers with a solid background in music theory and sight-singing are more confident in auditions and music rehearsals. They are valuable cast members because they are flexible, able to learn harmonies quickly, and delve into deeper work right away. There are so many aspects of the business of musical theatre that are out of your control as an actor, but being able to read music is not one of them. The process of learning to read can be fun but also challenging and frustrating at times. It is important to remember that it is worth it! This is the language of your field. You will be a better musician/performer/actor once you are able to fully understand and analyze the material of your chosen profession. Good luck and happy singing!

1

The Staff, Treble Clef, Pitches on the Staff, Solfege, and Sight-Singing

Music is written on a **staff**. The most commonly used staff in Western music is the five-line staff (seen below). Each staff has a **clef** to determine **pitch** (the highness or lowness of sound). The **treble clef** (𝄞), also known as the **G clef**, is used for higher-pitched instruments and voices. Practice drawing the treble clef on the staff.

Each line and space on the staff represents a different pitch. In music, pitch is designated by letter names (A, B, C, D, E, F, and G). When using a treble clef, the pitches of the lines and spaces are as follows:

It is important to remember that ascending pitches are in alphabetical order and descending pitches are in reverse alphabetical order. It is cyclical; once you get to G, start over again on A. If you know the English alphabet, you can figure out what pitch you are on.

Notice that the G is on the second line where the inner circle of the treble clef loops around. That is why the treble clef is also referred to as the G clef.

Notes are drawn on the staff to represent each pitch and its duration. Identify the following notes. The first two are done for you.

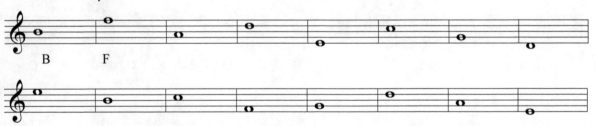

Draw the indicated notes. For each example there is more than one correct answer. The first two are done for you

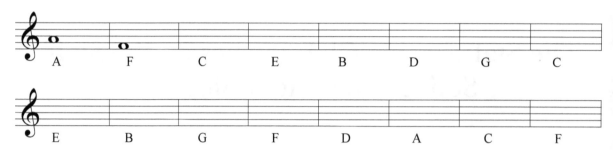

A   F   C   E   B   D   G   C

E   B   G   F   D   A   C   F

The location of the notes on the staff is directly related to the pitch where they are played or sung. A higher note on the staff sounds higher when played or sung. A lower note on the staff sounds lower.

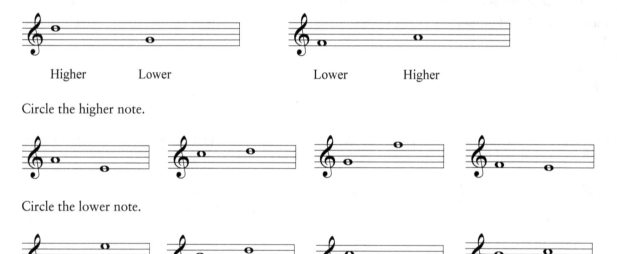

Higher   Lower   Lower   Higher

Circle the higher note.

Circle the lower note.

Go to listening example 1-1 to practice differentiating between high and low pitches.

Ledger lines are used to extend the staff in both directions. Ledger lines should be drawn with the same spacing as the lines on the staff.

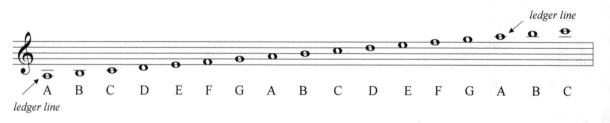

ledger line

A   B   C   D   E   F   G   A   B   C   D   E   F   G   A   B   C

ledger line

Draw *two* different notes of the same name. You may need to use ledger lines.

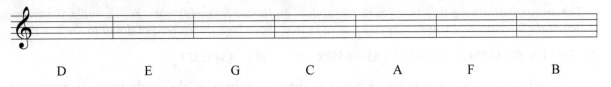

D   E   G   C   A   F   B

Sight-Singing

We are going to start sight-singing by looking at the C major **scale**. The C major scale starts and ends on C. All major scales have eight pitches. They are numbered 1–8, starting with the first pitch (these are called **scale degree** numbers). We will discuss more major scales in Chapter 3.

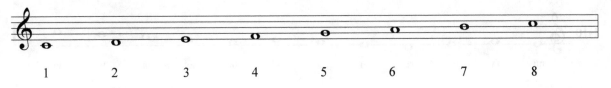

1   2   3   4   5   6   7   8

Listening example 1-2 is a C major scale played on the piano.

Practice singing the C major scale using the numbers as "words."

Once you are comfortable singing the pitches of the major scale using numbers, try adding **solfege**. Solfege is a system of syllables we will use for sight-singing. They provide a solid foundation once we move into more complex melodies.

If you are unfamiliar with solfege (or even if you are familiar with it), listen to "Do Re Mi" and the "Do-Re-Mi Encore" from *The Sound of Music* by Rodgers and Hammerstein. The entire song is based on solfege and has many clever word plays that will help you remember the syllables.

1 = do (doe)	5 = sol (so)
2 = re (ray)	6 = la (la)
3 = mi (me)	7 = ti (tea)
4 = fa (fa)	8 = do

Listen to the following exercises on the website. Practice singing along with the guide and then sing each example on your own.

Example 1-3: 12345678   87654321
You sing: do re mi fa sol la ti do   do ti la sol fa mi re do

Example 1-4: 12321   23432   34543   45654   56765   67876

Example 1-5: 123454321   234565432   345676543   456787654

Example 1-6: 876545678   765434567   654323456   543212345

Example 1-7: 12323434545656767878↑28   87676565454343232121↓71

The arrows indicate the direction your voice should go for the following note. For example, the arrow before the 2 means that you should go up to re (a step above high do) instead of down to the low re.

Example 1-8: 123434543   45434565   454565678   87656543   45432321

Sing each group of pitches using solfege. For each of these examples, C is "do" (scale degree 1). Again, you may sing along with each example on the website and then practice singing the exercises on your own.

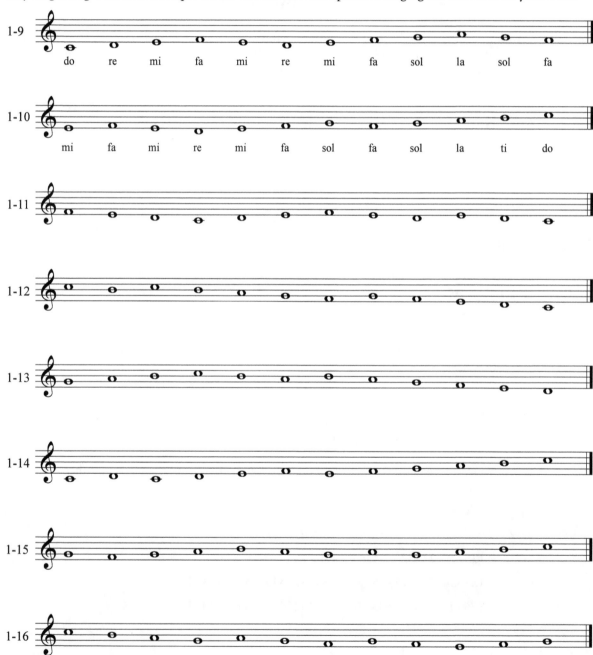

2

Rhythm: Whole Notes, Half Notes, Quarter Notes, and Eighth Notes

In addition to pitch, **rhythm** is another main component of music. Rhythm incorporates the duration of notes and rests as well as the accented patterns and beats that you hear in music.

American (British) Note Names

o = whole note (semibreve)   ♩ = quarter note (crotchet)   ♩ = half note (minim)   ♪ = eighth note (quaver)

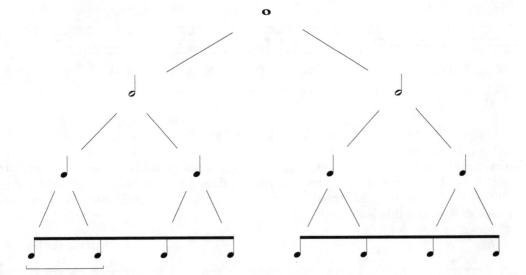

When eighth notes are next to each other, they are beamed together and look like this. Sometimes they are beamed together in groups of two and other times in groups of four. Either way, they hold the same value and are counted in the same manner.

> One whole note equals two half notes OR four quarter notes OR eight eighth notes.
> One half note equals two quarter notes OR four eighth notes.
> One quarter note equals two eighth notes.

All notes, with the exception of whole notes, are made up of two parts, the **note head** and the **stem**. When the stem is up, it is drawn on the right side of the note and when the stem is down, it is drawn on the left side of the note. Notes below the center line of the staff have stems going up and notes on or above the center line have stems going down.

Draw the indicated half notes ($\bigcirc$ / $\bigcirc$) on the staff.

A   E   C   D   F   B   G   E   C   F   A   D

Draw the indicated quarter notes ($\bullet$ / $\bullet$) on the staff.

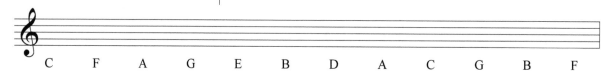

C   F   A   G   E   B   D   A   C   G   B   F

Time Signatures

The **time signature** at the beginning of the music signifies how the music will be grouped into **measures** (sometimes called **bars**). A measure is the space between two **bar lines**. There are different types of bar lines. Below you will find a single bar line and a final bar line. The final bar line signifies the end of the piece. Notice that it has two lines, one thin and one thick.

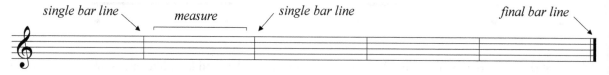

A time signature consists of two numbers. The top number tells you how many beats there will be in each measure and the bottom number identifies which note equals one beat.

time signature

The 4 on the top signifies that there are four beats in each measure.

The 4 on the bottom identifies that a quarter note equals one beat.

In 4/4 time, a quarter note (♩) equals 1 beat, therefore:

A half note (♪) = 2 beats   A whole note (o) = 4 beats   An eighth note (♪) = 1/2 beat

---

Add the values of each note to make sure you have four beats in each measure.

o = 4 beats = 1 measure   ♩ + ♩ = 4 beats = 1 measure

♩ + ♩ + ♩ + ♩ = 4 beats = 1 measure   ♪+♪+♪+♪+♪+♪+♪+♪ = 4 beats = 1 measure

Study the measures below to see how the different types of notes fit within each measure. **Listen** to example 2-1 to hear this exercise aloud.

    1 (2   3   4)   1   (2)   3   (4)   1   2   3   4   1   + 2   + 3   + 4   +

When counting eighth note rhythms, we use "and" (+) to signify the half beat.

The numbers in parentheses are silent beats. Even though a new note doesn't occur in this space, we need to observe the same amount of time to fill the measure.

Listen to example 2-2. Each measure can have any combination of notes as long as the values of the notes add up to four.

    1   2   + 3   4   1   2   3   (4)   1   (2)   3   + 4   +   1   (2   3   4)

Write the counts below the notes and then clap and count the rhythm. You can also **listen** to example 2-3 and practice clapping and counting with the recording.

Write the counts below the notes and then clap and count the rhythm. You can also **listen** to example 2-4 and practice clapping and counting with the recording.

HELPFUL HINTS

Get a **metronome**! A metronome is a device that provides a steady beat. It provides an audible beat (click, beep, or count) at a steady **tempo** (check out the performance tips in the review of Chapters 1–4 for more information about tempo). You can purchase a metronome at a local music store or get one as an app for your phone.

Once you have a metronome, set it to 70 bpm (beats per minute). Walk around the room to the beat; one step for each beat. Next, say the word "stage" on each beat. Once that is comfortable, say the word "broadway" on each beat, making both syllables equal in length. Alternate between "stage" and "broadway" as you walk and then add a clap to each syllable (one clap for "stage" and two claps for "broadway"). Once you are comfortable, try the exercises below. You can switch between using words and numbers to get the feel of the music. You can also listen to each example on the website.

Example 2-5

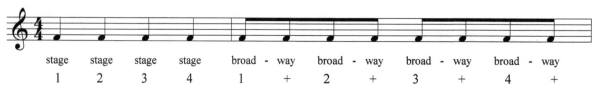

stage   stage   broad - way   broad - way   stage   broad - way   stage   broad - way
 1   2   3   +   4   +   1   2   +   3   4   +

Example 2-6

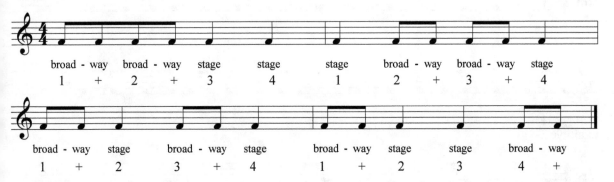

broad - way   broad - way   stage   stage   stage   broad - way   broad - way   stage
 1   +   2   +   3   4   1   2   +   3   +   4

broad - way   stage   broad - way   stage   broad - way   stage   stage   broad - way
 1   +   2   3   +   4   1   +   2   3   4   +

You can play around with this idea by finding other one- and two-syllable words. Put the words together to make a phrase and then write out the counts and the notes. Practice performing with your lyrics as well as clapping and counting the rhythmic patterns. Keep the metronome going to ensure that you are keeping a steady beat.

Try out this phrase:

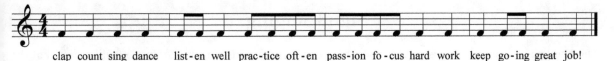

clap count sing dance   list-en well prac-tice oft-en pass-ion fo-cus hard work keep go-ing great job!

Now, clap and count the rhythm from this familiar song.

Harold Arlen
E.Y. Harburg

"Somewhere Over the Rainbow" from *The Wizard of Oz*

Some - where   o - ver the rain - bow,   way   up   high.
 1   (2)   3   (4)   1   2   +   3   4   1   (2)   3   (4)   1 (2 3 4)

There's   a   land   that I heard of   once   in a lul - la - by.
 1   (2)   3   (4)   1   2   +   3   4   1   2 + 3   4   1 (2 3 4)

Draw in the bar lines so that each measure has four beats. You should end up with eight measures total. Once the bar lines are drawn, write the counts below the notes and perform the rhythm by counting and clapping. Don't forget to use your metronome!

Example 2-7

Example 2-8

Example 2-8

Sight-Singing

The **one-line staff** seen below is used for non-pitched percussion instruments. Also, you will notice that the treble clef has been replaced by a small rectangle. This is a **percussion clef** (or rhythm clef), used for non-pitched instruments (like our hands).

Perform the following rhythmic examples by clapping and speaking the counts.

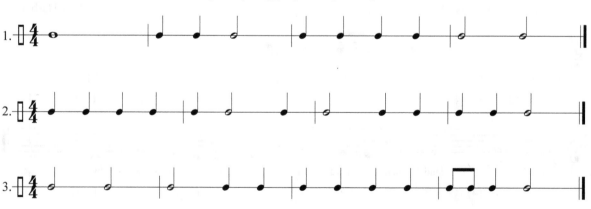

1. Perform each exercise by clapping and counting each rhythm.
2. Sing each exercise using solfege syllables and the correct rhythms.

3

The Piano Keyboard, Accidentals, Whole and Half Steps, Major Scales

The Keyboard

Each note on the staff correlates to a specific note on the piano **keyboard**. The keyboard is made up of black keys and white keys in a repeating pattern. The black keys are grouped in sets of two or three surrounded by three or four white keys respectively. Observe that "C" is always to the left of two black keys, while "F" is to the left of three black keys.

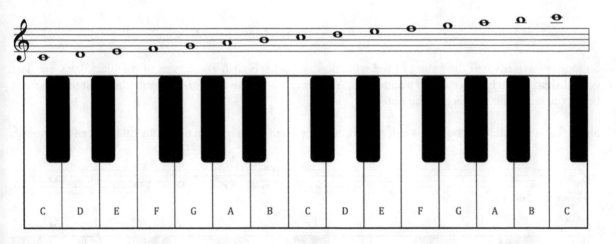

Intervals

An **interval** is the distance between two pitches. The smallest interval in traditional Western music is a **half step**. The distance between each adjacent note on the piano is a half step. Two half steps equal a **whole step**. Listen to example 3-1 to hear a few half steps and whole steps played on the piano.

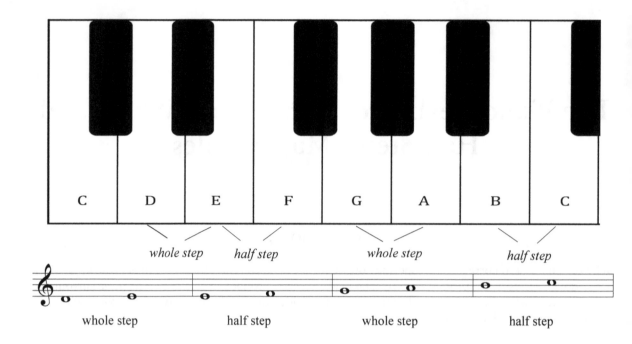

Accidentals

So far, we have covered the names of the white keys on a keyboard. The names of the black keys are **flats** (♭) and **sharps** (♯) which are called **accidentals**. Accidentals are drawn *before* the note on the staff and must be on the same line or space as the note.

Sharps raise the pitch of a note by a half step (remember a half step is the smallest interval between two notes).

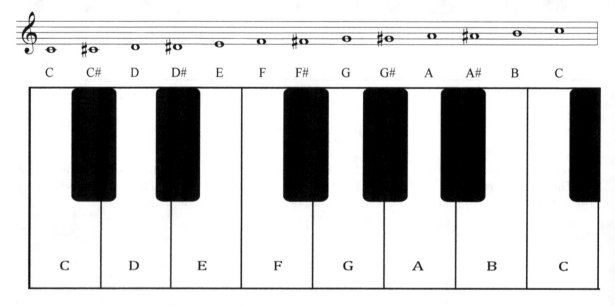

Flats lower the pitch of a note by a half step. A **natural** sign (♮) takes away the flat or sharp.

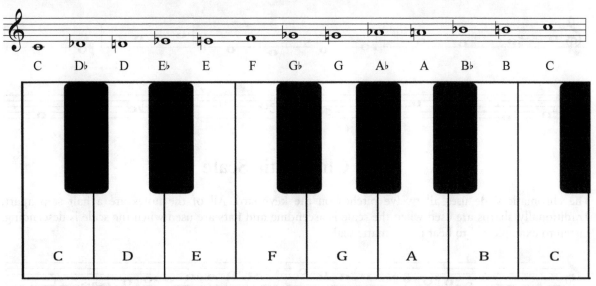

Remember that the smallest interval is a half step and that each adjacent note on the piano is a half step apart. Therefore, the distance between a white key and its adjacent black key is a half step.

Each of the black keys on a keyboard has two different names. Although each note has two names, the pitch sounds the same. These are called **enharmonic notes**.

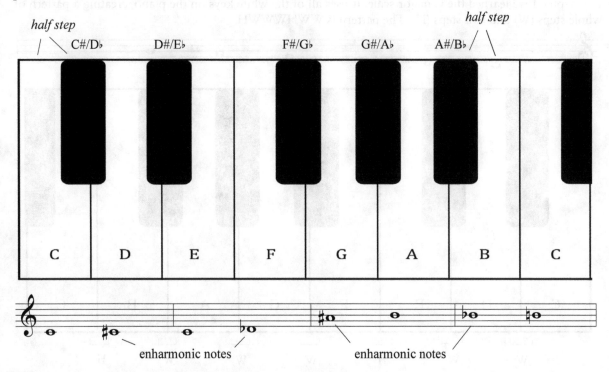

Listen to example 3-2 to hear these half steps.

Using the keyboard as a guide, identify each interval as a half step or a whole step.

The Chromatic Scale

The chromatic scale uses all twelve pitches on the keyboard. All of the notes are a half step apart. Traditionally, sharps are used when the scale is ascending and flats are used when the scale is descending. Listen to example 3-3 to hear a chromatic scale.

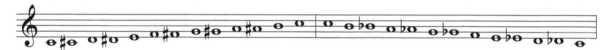

Major Scales

In Chapter 1 we learned the C major scale. It uses all of the white keys on the piano, creating a pattern of whole steps (W) and half steps (H). The pattern is WWHWWWH.

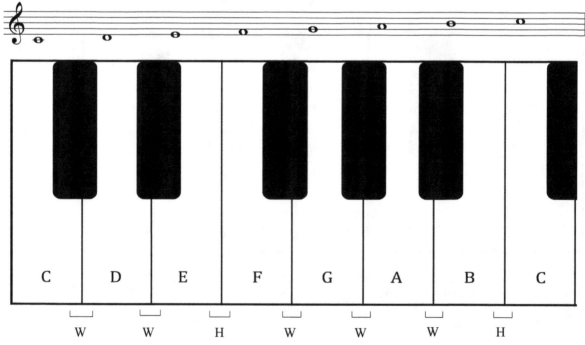

Using the pattern (WWHWWWH), you can create a major scale starting on any note. The pattern for a major scale is always the same, no matter what starting pitch you choose. Therefore, the interval from the first note of the scale ("do") to the second ("re") or the third ("mi") to the fifth ("fa") is the same in all major scales. Based on this idea, we can **transpose** music into different keys and the melody still sounds the same. You will need to use accidentals (sharps and flats) to make the pattern work for each scale.

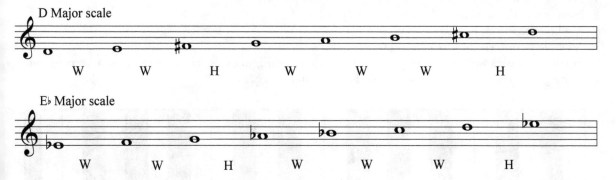

Check these scales on the keyboard to see how the pattern works.

Steps for drawing a major scale:

1. Draw the first note (the name of the scale). Make sure you use an accidental if necessary.

E major scale

2. Draw the remaining seven notes, ending on the same note name you started on. Make sure you have one note on each line and space in between your starting and ending notes.

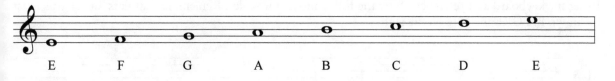

3. Use the WWHWWWH pattern to add the appropriate accidentals.

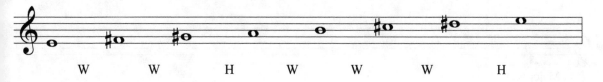

How did we get there?

1. Start with your finger on E on the keyboard below.

2. Now we need to move up a whole step. E–F is only a half step but if you add a # to the F, you get a whole step.

3. Starting on F#, go up another whole step. You land on G#.

4. From G# you need to go up a half step, which gets you to A.

5. Next is a whole step from A, bringing you to B.

6. A whole step from B brings you up to C#.

7. A whole step from C# gets you to D#.

8. Finally, you end with a half step up to E. If your ending pitch is different than your starting pitch, something has gone wrong and you should go back and try again.

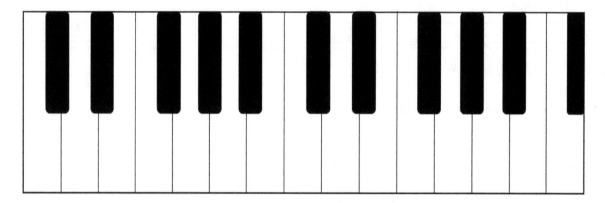

Remember these rules for major scales:

1. Every scale must use each of the seven pitch letters.

2. Do not mix flats and sharps in one scale.

3. Follow the WWHWWWH pattern.

4. The ascending scale has eight notes. It starts and ends on the same note.

Using the keyboard as a reference, draw the following major scales. Remember that flats and sharps must be drawn BEFORE the note on the staff.

B♭ Major scale

F♯ Major scale

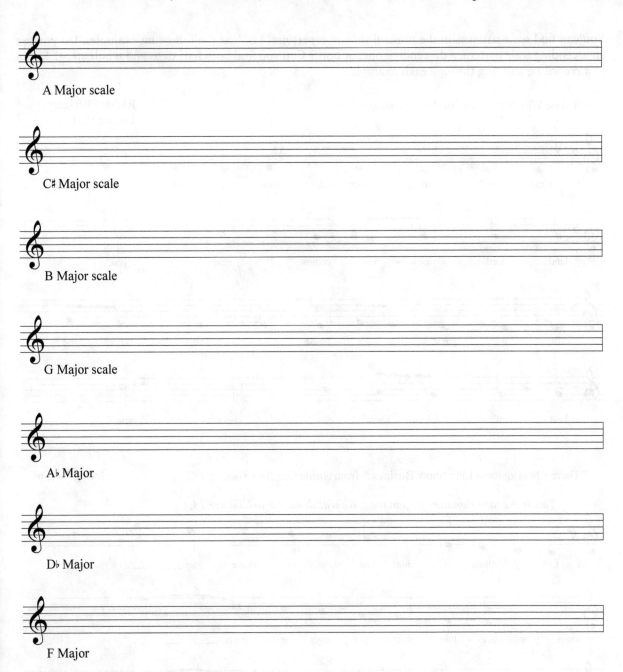

A Major scale

C# Major scale

B Major scale

G Major scale

A♭ Major

D♭ Major

F Major

You can find scale patterns in the musical theatre repertoire. Look at the following examples. Do you see an ascending scale pattern, a descending one, or both? Can you find both half steps and whole steps? Listen to a recording and sing through each example.

"Come With Me" from *The Boys From Syracuse*   Richard Rodgers
Lorenz Hart

Come with me where the food is free Where the land - lord ne - ver comes near you. Be a guest in a house of rest, Where the best of fel - lows can cheer you.

"There's No Business Like Show Business" from *Annie Get Your Gun*   Irving Berlin

This is the time signature for cut time. We will discuss it in Chapter 13.

Ev' ry thing in - side you starts to shake up____ when your pic - ture in the news ap - pears.____ And the thrill each morn - ing when you wake up____ with daubs of make - up be - hind your ears.

Song Analysis

What role do the scale patterns play in each of these excerpts?

In "Come With Me," you start on middle "c" and the **phrase** (musical sentence) rises using whole steps and half steps until you get to the "a" on the lyric "near you." The next phrase also begins on middle "c" but this time ascends all the way to high "c." Ascending lines are often building towards something. When you combine the lyrics with the ascending line, you can see that the singer is trying to convince someone to come with him. In this case the Sergeant is convincing Antipholus to go to jail. The ascending lines convey the importance of the message as well as the intensity in which the message is being delivered. The second phrase ascends higher and raises the stakes in case Antipholus wasn't convinced after the first phrase.

In "There's No Business Like Show Business," you have three ascending scale lines with the final one continuing to a "d" before descending to an "a" at the end of the phrase. Each line is building suspense and excitement until we get to the climax on "make-up." This opening number is engaging the audience by sharing the joy and exhilaration of putting on a show. Each ascending line is almost saying "there is more—and this and this—but wait until this!"

Take a look and a listen to the following songs as well:

"Babes in Arms" from *Babes in Arms* by Rodgers and Hart.

> The melody slowly builds all the way up the scale as the young people come together to fight for what they believe.

"Oklahoma!" from *Oklahoma!* by Rodgers and Hammerstein.

> Look for descending scale patterns and large ascending jumps that create excitement.

Sight-Singing

Sing the following melodies using solfege while keeping a steady beat.

Listening

Listen to example 3-4 and determine if you are hearing a half step or a whole step.

A. half step	7.	15.
B. whole step	8.	16.
1.	9.	17.
2.	10.	18.
3.	11.	19.
4.	12.	20.
5.	13.	21.
6.	14.	22

4

The Circle of Fifths and Major Key Signatures

Major Keys

There are fifteen major keys in Western music. The key is indicated by the grouping of flats or sharps found on the staff next to the clef. This is called the **key signature**. The accidentals that make up the key signature are carried through the entire piece or until there is a change in the key. Therefore, it is unnecessary to write accidentals in front of the notes throughout the piece of music.

Major keys are divided into sharp keys and flat keys except for C major. As we know from the C major scale, there are no sharps or flats in C major.

The Sharp Keys

The sharp keys are as follows (the order is based on the number of sharps in the key): G (1 sharp), D (2 sharps), A (3 sharps), E (4 sharps), B (5 sharps), F♯ (6 sharps), C♯ (7 sharps). (See the **circle of fifths** below.) The circle is a tool to visualize the relationships between major keys. The sharp keys appear clockwise around the circle. Each key is a fifth higher than the key before it. A fifth is an interval made up of seven half steps.

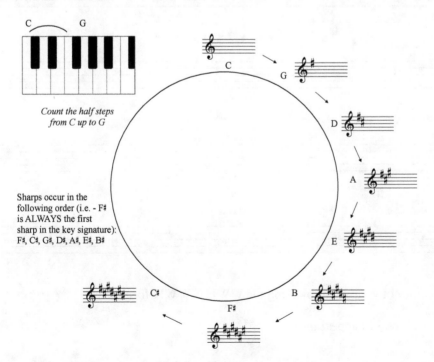

Count the half steps from C up to G

Sharps occur in the following order (i.e. - F♯ is ALWAYS the first sharp in the key signature): F♯, C♯, G♯, D♯, A♯, E♯, B♯

Identify the following key signatures.

Draw a treble clef in each measure along with the indicated key signature.

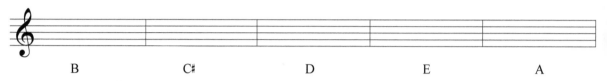

B   C♯   D   E   A

Draw the following major scales using the appropriate key signature. To draw a scale, draw the key signature first. Next, draw the first note of the scale. The first note is the name of the key. Finally, draw seven notes ascending up the staff, one on each line or space. The final note should be the same as the first note. You should have eight notes in total.

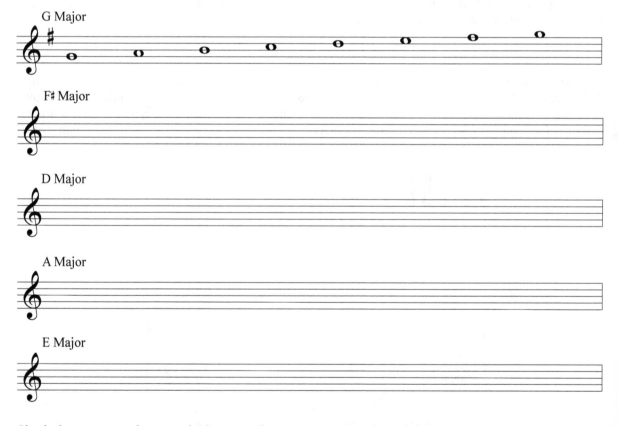

G Major

F♯ Major

D Major

A Major

E Major

Check the accuracy of your scales by using the WWHWWWH formula.

List the sharps in order of appearance:

_____   _____   _____   _____   _____   _____   _____

The Flat Keys

The flat keys are as follows (the order is based on the number of flats in the key): F (1 flat), B♭ (2 flats), E♭ (3 flats), A♭ (4 flats), D♭ (5 flats), G♭ (6 flats), C♭ (7 flats).
See the circle of fifths below. The flat keys appear counter-clockwise around the circle. Each key is a fifth lower than key before it.

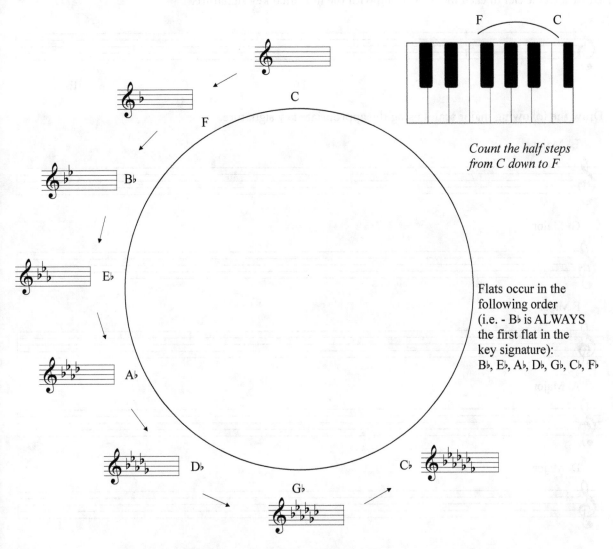

*Count the half steps
from C down to F*

Flats occur in the
following order
(i.e. - B♭ is ALWAYS
the first flat in the
key signature):
B♭, E♭, A♭, D♭, G♭, C♭, F♭

Identify the following key signatures.

Draw a treble clef in each measure along with the indicated key signature.

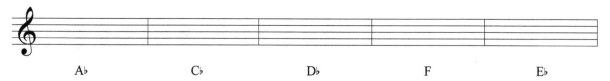

Draw the following major scales using the appropriate key signature.

Check the accuracy of your scales by using the WWHWWWH formula.

List the flats in order of appearance:

____   ____   ____   ____   ____   ____   ____

THE COMPLETE CIRCLE OF FIFTHS

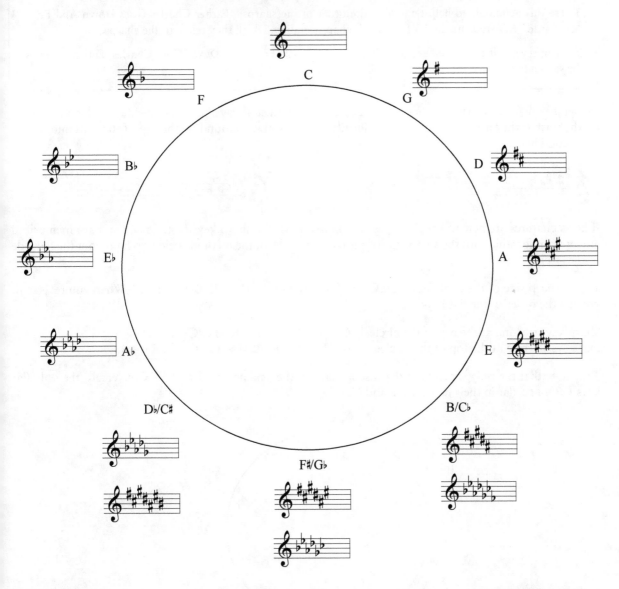

Enharmonic Keys: B and C♭ are enharmonic keys. The notes in each key are the same but are spelled differently. Using a keyboard, compare the notes in the scales. They are exactly the same.

IN ADDITION—F♯ major is enharmonic to G♭ major and D♭ major is enharmonic to C♯ major.

HELPFUL HINTS

Use this neumonic to help remember the order of the sharps: "Father Charles Goes Down And Ends Battle." My students think of this as the happy ending, which they relate to the sharps.

You can reverse it to remember the order of flats: "Battle Ends And Down Goes Charles' Father." This is the sad ending, which they relate to the flats.

Remember that the sharps and flats in the key signature must always be in the specified order and appear on the staff as they are drawn below. Specifically, the G♯ is always found on the top of the staff and not on the second line.

If key signatures are new to you, I suggest working on just the sharp keys first. Once you have memorized and are comfortable with the sharp side of the circle, try one of the methods below to figure out the flat side of the circle.

1. The sharp side of the circle starts on C and follows with G, D, A, E, B, F♯, and C♯. When you reverse it, you get the order of the flat keys.

Sharp keys starting at the top of the circle: C G D A E B F♯ C♯
Flat keys starting at the top of the circle: C F B♭ E♭ A♭ D♭ G♭ C♭

Take note that the only sharp keys that use a sharp in their name are F♯ and C♯. Conversely, the only flat keys *without* a flat in their name are F and C.

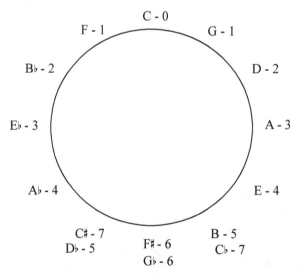

2. If you add the number of sharps in any sharp key to the number of flats in the flat key with the same letter name, it will add up to 7, i.e. G major has 1 sharp and G♭ major has 6 flats. B major has 5 sharps and B♭ major has 2 flats.

One additional way to check if your key signature is correct is to go back to the pattern for major scales. The accidentals you add in the scale should be the same as the accidentals found in the key signature.

For example, draw an A♭ major scale using the WWHWWWH pattern.

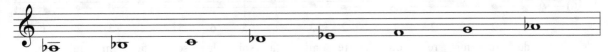

You end up with 4 flats (well actually 5, but you don't count the A♭ twice)—A♭, B♭, D♭, and E♭.

Does the key of A♭ have 4 flats? Yes, it does! The key signature and scale match.

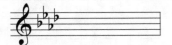   B♭, E♭, A♭, and D♭

Now draw a B major scale using the WWHWWWH pattern.

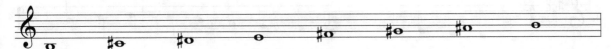

You end up with 5 sharps—C♯, D♯, F♯, G♯, and A♯.

Does the key of B have 5 sharps? Yes, it does! The key signature and scale match.

   F♯, C♯, G♯, D♯, and A♯

Sight-Singing

When singing in any major key, the **tonic,** or first note of the scale, is always "do." Look at the D major scale, which is labeled with the scale degree numbers and the corresponding solfege. Sing the scale and then the following melody.

Determine the key signature for each exercise and write out the scale degree numbers and corresponding solfege syllables below. Remember that the tonic is always "do." Practice by singing a major scale in each key before singing each melody.

Now, practice singing the following exercises without writing in all of the solfege syllables. Make sure you check the key signature before you start!

Review of Chapters 1–4 and Performance Tips (Tempo)

Note Recognition

Identify the following notes.

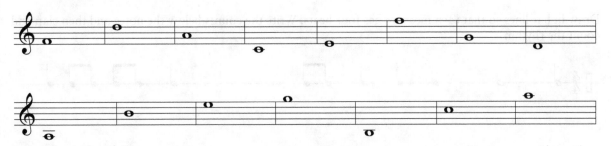

Draw *two* different notes of the same name. You may need to use ledger lines.

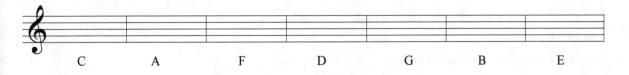

| C | A | F | D | G | B | E |

Rhythm

Draw the following notes. In 4/4 time, what is the value of each note?

whole note:

half note:

quarter note:

eighth note:

Fill each measure with the type of notes indicated. Make sure there are four beats in each measure.

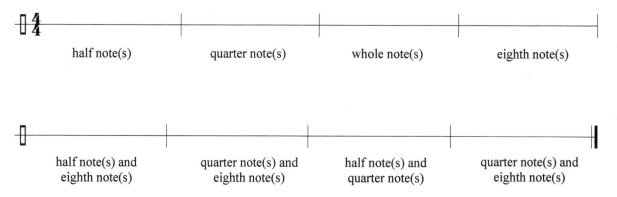

half note(s)   quarter note(s)   whole note(s)   eighth note(s)

half note(s) and   quarter note(s) and   half note(s) and   quarter note(s) and
eighth note(s)   eighth note(s)   quarter note(s)   eighth note(s)

Draw in bar lines so that each measure has four beats. Write the counts below the notes and then clap and count the rhythm.

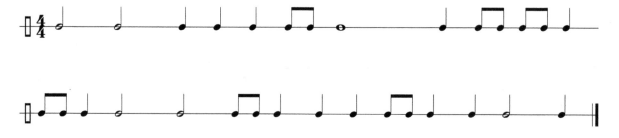

Write the counts below the notes and then perform the rhythm.

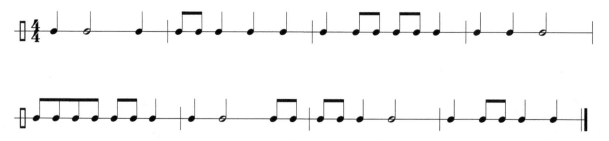

The Keyboard

Write the note names on the keyboard. Be sure to identify all of the white keys as well as all of the black keys.

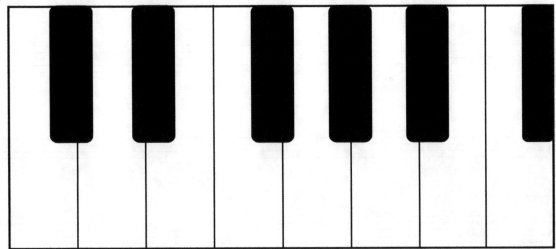

Intervals

Identify each interval as a whole step or a half step.

Major Scales

Using the pattern WWHWWWH, draw the following major scales with accidentals (not a key signature).

E Major

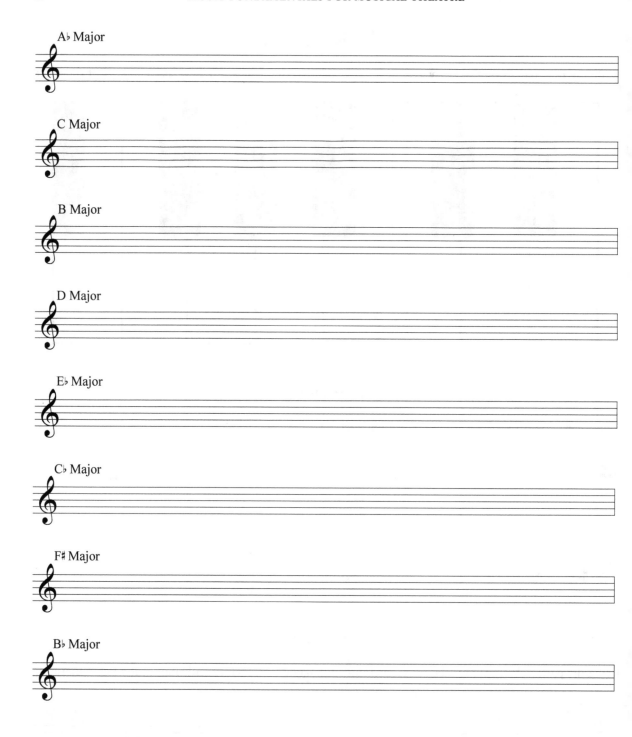

A♭ Major

C Major

B Major

D Major

E♭ Major

C♭ Major

F♯ Major

B♭ Major

C# Major

F Major

G♭ Major

G Major

D♭ Major

A Major

Major Key Signatures

What is the order of the sharps?
What is the order of the flats?

Draw a complete circle of fifths.

Draw a treble clef in each measure along with the indicated key signature.

| D | E | B | G | F♯ | A |

| A♭ | B♭ | F | D♭ | E♭ | G♭ |

HELPFUL HINTS

Sharp key signatures: When you see a sharp key signature, take the last sharp and raise it a half step to get the name of the key, i.e. if the key signature has two sharps, F♯ and C♯, take the C♯ and think up a half step. You come to D, which is the name of the key.

Flat key signatures: When you see a flat key signature, look at the second to last flat. That is the name of the key, i.e. if the key signature has four flats, B♭, E♭, A♭, D♭, look at the second to last flat. A♭ is the name of the key.

Sight-Singing

Determine the major key for each exercise and then sing it using solfege while keeping a steady beat. You may need to write the scale degree numbers or solfege syllables under the notes. As you become more comfortable with sight-singing, try a few exercises without writing out the solfege.

Performance Tips

The ability to read pitches and rhythms is only part of the knowledge you need to read music. You will encounter many markings in your music that give you directions on how to perform the music. With these markings, the composer gives you insight as to how they intended the music to be performed. Look at music that you are currently working on—can you find any of these markings?

Tempo (Speed in Music)

The speed of a piece of music is measured in **beats per minutes** (bpm). A **metronome** is an extremely helpful tool to measure beats per minute. It will keep a steady tempo for you at any speed. You can purchase one at a local music store or get one as an app for your phone. Some metronomes will also subdivide the beat for you, giving you steady eighth notes or sixteenth notes.

At the beginning of your music you will often see a tempo marking. The tempo marking may be one of the terms below or a bpm notation like this: ♩ = 120. This notation tells you that the speed of each quarter note should be 120 bpm.

Tempo markings are usually found at the beginning of a piece or at new section of music. You will find a variety of descriptive tempo markings in musical theatre. The terms listed below are the most traditional:

Largo: very slowly or broadly (45–50 bpm)
Adagio: slow and stately (55–65 bpm)
Andante : walking tempo (84–90 bpm)
Moderato: moderately (100–112 bpm)
Allegro: quick or brightly (120–160 bpm)
Presto: extremely fast (180–200 bpm)

Tempo alterations are markings that indicate a change in the tempo:

Accelerando (*accel.*): gradually speed up

Ritardando (*rit.*): slow down

Rallentando (*rall.*): gradually slow down

*ritardando and rallentando are often used interchangeably.

a tempo: back to the original tempo

rubato: rhythmic freedom for a short period of time—gives the performer liberty to slow down and/or speed up in an expressive manner

colla voce: with the voice (the accompanist or orchestra follows the singer for the indicated passage)

meno mosso: with more motion

piu mosso: with less motion

5

Intervals: Seconds and Thirds and Phrase Shapes

Intervals

As we discussed in Chapter 3, an **interval** is the distance between two pitches. We measure the distance covered with numbers, just like measuring height or weight. In this book we will cover seconds, thirds, fourths, fifths, sixths, sevenths, unisons, and octaves. See an example of each below.

Let's start by looking at **seconds** and **thirds**.

How many letters (note names) are there when traveling from C to D?

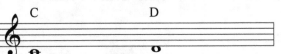

Two note names from C to D means that the distance traveled (interval) is a **second.**

How many letters (note names) are there when traveling from C to E?

Three note names from C to E means that the distance traveled the distance traveled (interval) is a **third.**

Here are a few more examples of seconds and thirds. Notice that when we are counting letter names, we don't treat a flat or sharp any differently than a natural note.

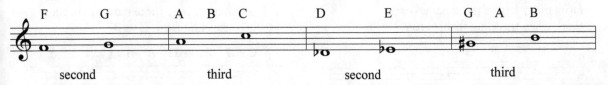

Now, count the notes and label the intervals as seconds or thirds.

We can use the same process of counting letter names to identify **fourths**, **fifths**, **sixths**, and **sevenths**.

How many letters (note names) are there when traveling from C to F?

Four note names from C to F means that the distance traveled (interval) is a **fourth.**

How many letters (note names) are there when traveling from C to G?

Five note names from C to G means that the distance traveled (interval) is a **fifth.**

Count the notes and label the intervals as fourths or fifths. The first two have been done for you.

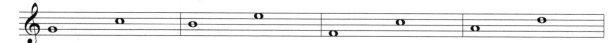

How many letters (note names) are there when traveling from C to A?

Six note names from C to A means that the distance traveled (interval) is a **sixth.**

How many letters (note names) are there when traveling from C to B?

Seven note names from C to B means that the distance traveled (interval) is a **seventh.**

Count the notes and label the intervals as sixths or sevenths. The first two have been done for you.

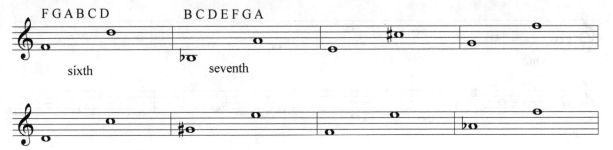

Major and Minor Intervals

In this chapter we will focus on major and minor seconds and thirds. As we just learned, a second is the distance between any two adjacent notes on the staff. The number of half steps separating these two notes is what makes the interval major or minor.

Both C–D♭ and C–D are seconds because they are adjacent notes on the staff. Using the keyboard below, count the number of half steps in between the two notes.

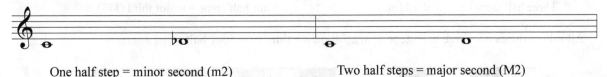

One half step = minor second (m2)   Two half steps = major second (M2)

All minor seconds are one half step apart. All major seconds are two half steps apart.

Intervals can begin on any note. Take a look at the following seconds and then listen to example 5-1 to hear them played on the piano.

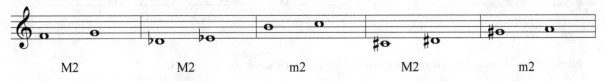

Notice the abbreviation for major second is M2 and for minor second it is m2.

Label the following seconds. The first two are done for you.

You can also determine whether a third is major or minor by counting the number of half steps separating the two notes.

Both C–E♭ and C–E are thirds because we travel through three note names to get from C–E. Using the keyboard below, count the number of half steps in between the two notes.

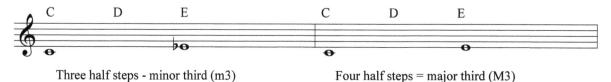

Three half steps - minor third (m3)   Four half steps = major third (M3)

All minor thirds are three half steps apart. All major thirds are four half steps apart.

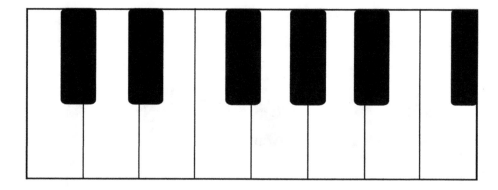

Take a look at the following thirds and then listen to example 5-2 to hear them played on the piano.

Notice the abbreviation for major third is M3 and for minor third it is m3.

Label the following thirds. The first two are done for you.

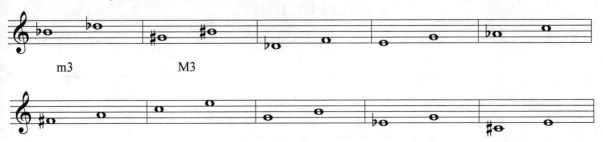

      m3   M3

When drawing intervals, it is helpful to think about it as a two-step process. First, draw the basic interval and then figure out if the top note needs to be natural, flat, or sharp based on the number of half steps. This will ensure that you are spelling the third correctly and not using the incorrect enharmonic spelling. (i.e. writing a D♯ when it should be an E♭). You can accomplish this by using the letter names of the notes to help. See below:

1. To draw a major third above the given note, write out three letter names starting with the given note.
2. Count up four half steps (using the keyboard to help) and add an accidental if necessary.

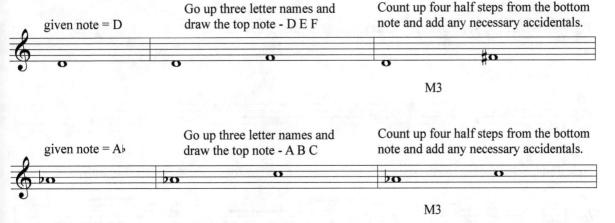

Follow the same process for a minor third except that you need to count three half steps instead of four.

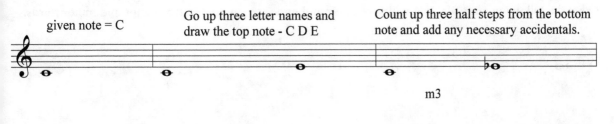

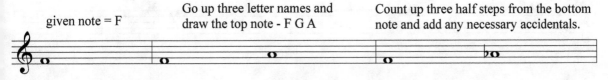

HELPFUL HINTS

Whaen counting half steps, make sure you count the distance between the notes, not the notes themselves.

Draw a major third above each note.

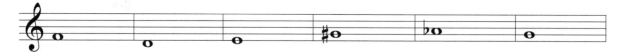

Draw a minor third above each note.

Circle and label all of the thirds in the following melody. Sing through the melody using solfege.

Label the following intervals. You will find major and minor seconds as well as major and minor thirds.

You will find many thirds in the musical theatre repertoire. Look at the following examples and label the thirds. Listen to a recording and sing through each song.

"Hello!" from *The Book Of Mormon*

Trey Parker
Robert Lopez
Matt Stone

Song Analysis

Melodic musical phrases have a shape. The shape of the phrase gives the actor clues to the state of mind of the character and what the character's objective might be. Some **phrase shapes** are:

Look at the first four bars of "Maybe." The phrase goes up to the "d" and then comes down to the "f." To me, the first part of the phrase supports the initial excitement and build-up of Annie's hope of finding her parents. The second part of the phrase seems more thoughtful, or reasoning. Of course, each actor can interpret the phrase shape in her own way, but it is important to remember that these details are there to help tell the story.

Now, look at "As Long As He Needs Me." Here the phrases start high and go down until the final two-bar phrase where the notes move in an upward direction. The descending phrases can be felt like sighs. She is building her thoughts to the strong declaration at the end, "I'm sure that he needs me."

Analyze the phrase shapes in music that you are working on or any of the excerpts in the book. Use the shapes to further your investigation into the character and performance of the music.

Take a look and listen to the following songs as well. Find the phrases and analyze the intervals. Sing each song using solfege.

"Home" from *Beauty and the Beast*.
"Miracle of Miracles" from *Fiddler On The Roof*.
"Hold On" from *The Secret Garden*.
"Tune Up A" from *Rent*.

Sight-Singing

Sing the following pattern using solfege.

1324354657687↑28 8675645342312↓71   ***sing this every day!***

Sing the following melodies using solfege while keeping a steady beat. Make sure you check the key signature before starting each exercise. You can listen to the first three melodies on the website for reference.

Example 5-3

Example 5-4

Example 5-5

Listening

Listen to example 5-6 and determine if you are hearing a major third or a minor third.

A. major third	5.	11.
B. minor third	6.	12.
1.	7.	13.
2.	8.	14.
3.	9.	15.
4.	10.	16.

Listen to example 5-7 and identify the interval you are hearing. Is it a major second, minor second, major third or minor third?

A. major third	7.	15.
B. minor second	8.	16.
1.	9.	17.
2.	10.	18.
3.	11.	19.
4.	12.	20.
5.	13.	21.
6.	14.	22.

Listen to example 5-8 and write out the rhythm that you hear.

Listen to example 5-9 and write out the rhythm that you hear.

6

Intervals: Fourths, Fifths, and Octaves; Rhythm: Sixteenth Notes

Perfect Intervals

Fourths, fifths, and **octaves** are considered **perfect** intervals. They are never major or minor but can be altered to become augmented or diminished. We will discuss that in a later chapter.

We can identify perfect fourths and fifths by counting the number of half steps separating the two notes.

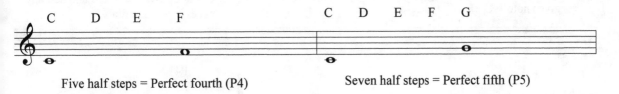

Five half steps = Perfect fourth (P4)   Seven half steps = Perfect fifth (P5)

All perfect fourths are five half steps apart. All perfect fifths are seven half steps apart.

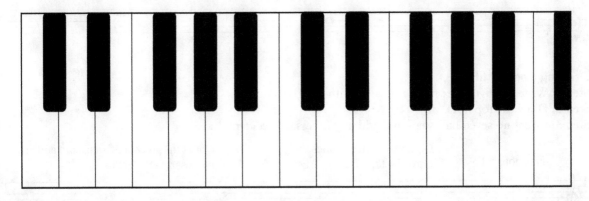

Below are a few examples of perfect fourths and fifths. Listen to example 6-1 to hear them played on the piano.

P4   P4   P5   P5

Label the following perfect fourths and perfect fifths. The first two are done for you.

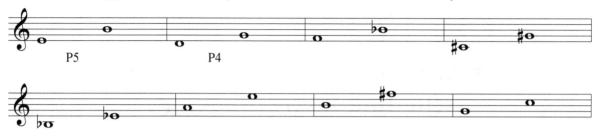

We use the same two-step process to draw perfect fourths and perfect fifths as we did for thirds.

Drawing a **perfect fourth**:
Step 1: Write out four letter names starting with the given note.
Step 2: Draw the top note.
Step 3: Count up five half steps and add any necessary accidentals.

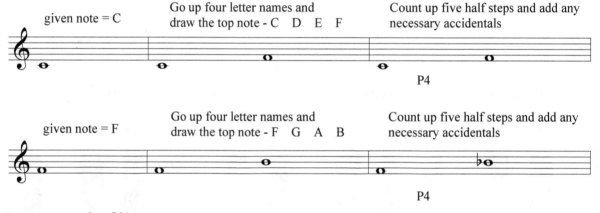

Drawing a **perfect fifth**:
Step 1: Write out five letter names starting with the given note.
Step 2: Draw the top note.
Step 3: Count up seven half steps and add any necessary accidentals.

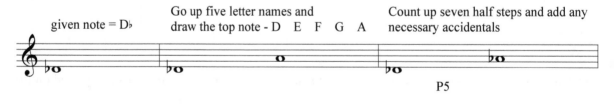

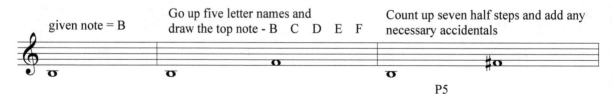

An **octave**, or perfect eighth, is the same note (same letter name), twelve half steps apart.

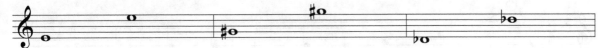

Draw a perfect fourth above each note.

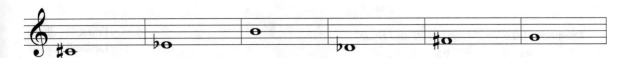

Draw a perfect fifth above each note.

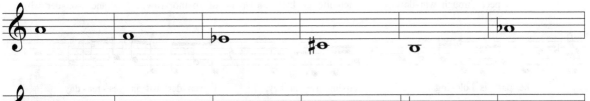

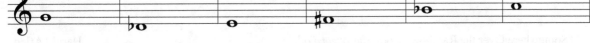

Draw a perfect eighth (octave) above each note.

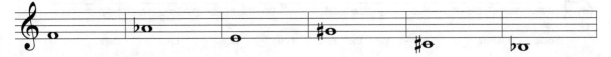

Find and label the perfects fourths, fifths, and octaves in the following song excerpts. Listen to a recording and sing each excerpt.

"Comedy Tonight" from *A Funny Thing Happened on the Way to the Forum*   Stephen Sondheim

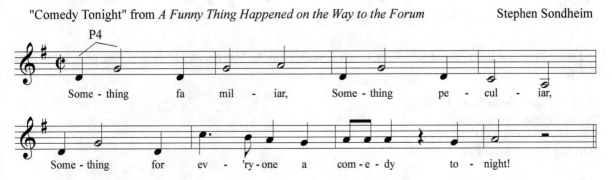

"My Favorite Things" from *The Sound of Music* — Richard Rodgers, Oscar Hammerstein

Rain drops on ros - es and whisk - ers on kit - tens,
bright cop - per ket - tles and warm wool - en mit - tens

"Someone Like You" from *Jekyll and Hyde* — Frank Wildhorn, Leslie Bricusse

I peer through win-dows, watch life go by. Dream of to-mor-row ___ and won-der why
the past is hold-ing me, ___ keep-ing life at bay. I wan-der lost in yes - ter - day

"Somewhere Over the Rainbow" from *The Wizard of Oz* — Harold Arlen, E.Y. Harburg

Some - where o - ver the rain - bow, way up high.
There's a land that I heard of once in a lul - la - by.

Take a look and listen to the following songs as well. Find the fourths and fifths and sing each song using solfege.

"I Met A Girl" from *Bells Are Ringing*.
"Some People" from *Gypsy*.
"World's Greatest Dad" from *Elf*.
"On My Own" from *Les Miserables*.

Rhythm

Sixteenth notes (♪) are worth half the value of an eighth note.

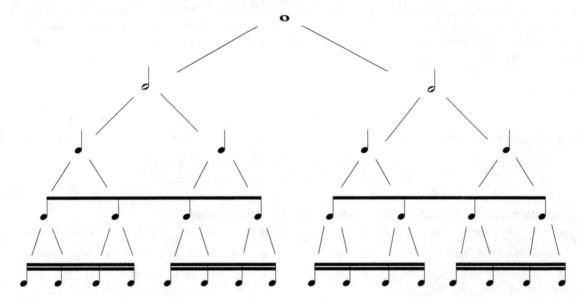

Therefore, if an eighth note is worth half a beat in 4/4 time, a sixteenth note is worth a quarter of a beat.

♪+♪+♪+♪+♪+♪+♪+♪+♪+♪+♪+♪+♪+♪+♪+♪ = 4 beats = 1 measure

A group of four sixteenth notes can be counted # (the number of the beat)—e (eee)—+ (and)—a (ah).

Keeping a steady beat, practice clapping and counting the following exercise out loud. Listen to example 6-2 to hear a performance of this excerpt.

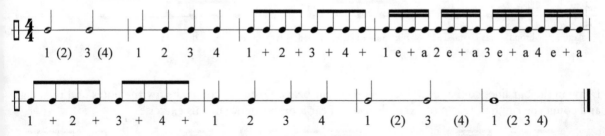

Write the counts below the notes and then clap and count the rhythm. Listen to example 6-3 to hear a performance of this excerpt.

Remember in Chapter 2 we used words to help understand rhythm? Let's revisit that idea for sixteenth notes. Set your metronome to 70 bpm and walk around the room to the beat. Begin to clap on the beat as well. Once the beat is set in your body, add the word "stage" on every quarter note. Eventually move into eighth notes by speaking the word "broad-way." Lastly, move into sixteenth notes, speaking the phrase "big au-di-tion." You should use one syllable on each sixteenth note. Alternate between quarter notes, eighth notes, and sixteenth notes until you feel confident in the different patterns. You can use the following exercises as a guide.

Example 6-4

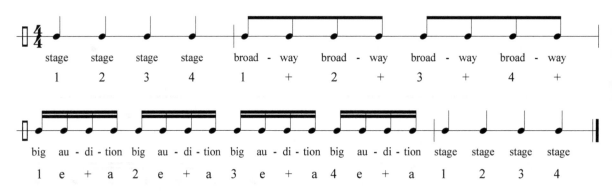

Example 6-5

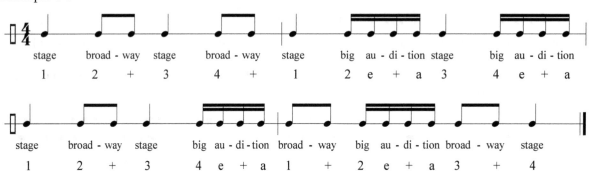

Draw in the bar lines so that each measure has four beats. Write the counts below the notes and then clap and count the rhythm. Listen to example 6-6 to hear a performance of this exercise.

Write the counts below the notes and then clap and count the rhythm.

In addition to four sixteenth notes in a row, you will find other sixteenth note patterns that also add up to one beat. The following patterns combine two sixteenth notes with one eighth note. Listen to example 6-7 to hear this exercise.

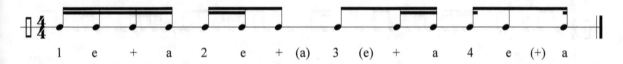

Practice each sixteenth note pattern with a metronome. Use the following exercise to work on jumping from one pattern to the next while keeping a steady beat. Listen to example 6-8 to hear this exercise.

Draw in the bar lines so that each measure has four beats. Write the counts below the notes and then clap and count the rhythm. Listen to example 6-9 to hear a performance of this exercise.

Write the counts below the notes and then clap and count the rhythm.

Sight-Singing

Sing the following melodies using solfege while keeping a steady beat.

Listening

Listen to example 6-10 and write the rhythm that you hear.

Listen to example 6-11 and write the rhythm that you hear.

Listen to example 6-12 and write the rhythm that you hear.

Listen to example 6-13 and determine if you are hearing a perfect fourth, a perfect fifth or an octave.

A. perfect fourth	4.	10.
B. perfect fifth	5.	11.
C. octave	6.	12.
1.	7.	13.
2.	8.	14.
3.	9.	15.

Listen to example 6-14 and determine the interval you are hearing. Is it a major or minor second, a major or minor third, a perfect fourth, fifth, or octave?

1.	9.	17.
2.	10.	18.
3.	11.	19.
4.	12.	20.
5.	13.	21.
6.	14.	22.
7.	15.	23.
8.	16.	24.

7

Intervals: Sixths and Sevenths; Rhythm: Rests

And More Intervals

In this chapter, we will focus on **major** and **minor sixths** as well as **major** and **minor sevenths**. Let's take a look at sixths first.

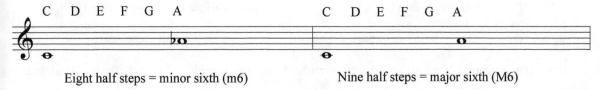

All minor sixths are eight half steps apart. All major sixths are nine half steps apart.

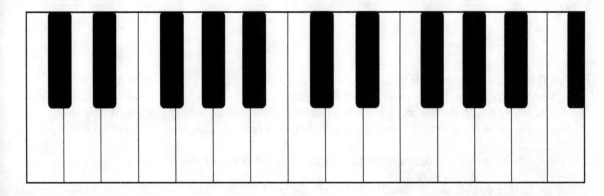

Below are a few examples of minor and major sixths. Listen to example 7-1 to hear them played on the piano.

Label the following minor and major sixths. The first two are done for you.

Now, let's look at sevenths.

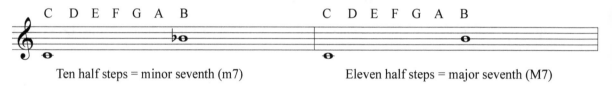

Ten half steps = minor seventh (m7)   Eleven half steps = major seventh (M7)

All minor sevenths are ten half steps apart. All major sevenths are eleven half steps apart.

Below are a few examples of minor and major sevenths. Listen to example 7-2 to hear them played on the piano.

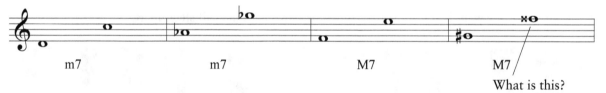

What is this?

The ✗ symbolizes a **double sharp**. Instead of writing two sharps on the staff, we use an ✗. A double sharp raises the pitch by two half steps. In this case, we are raising the F by two half steps. If you look at the piano, you should now be on a G. F double sharp is an enharmonic spelling of G. In this example it is written as an F double sharp because F is seven note names from the bottom note G#, which creates the interval of a seventh.

Label the following minor and major sevenths. The first two are done for you.

Here we have a **double flat**. A double flat lowers the pitch by two half steps. We do not have a special symbol for a double flat. You simply put two flats in front of the note.

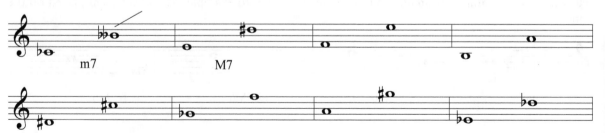

Identify and label the following intervals.

We use the same two-step process to draw minor and major sixths and sevenths as we did for the other intervals.

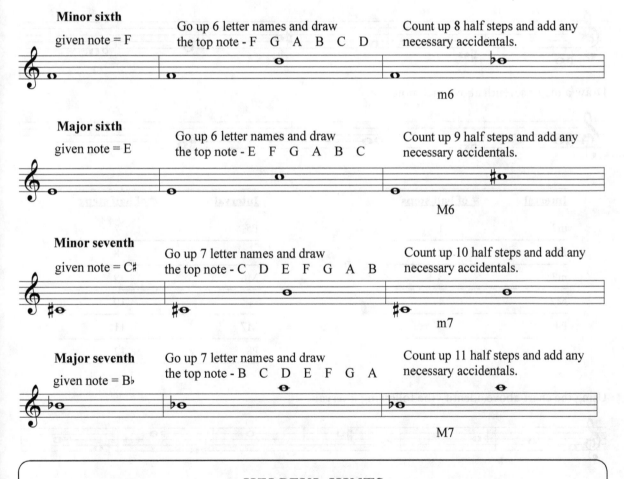

Minor sixth

given note = F

Go up 6 letter names and draw the top note - F G A B C D

Count up 8 half steps and add any necessary accidentals.

m6

Major sixth

given note = E

Go up 6 letter names and draw the top note - E F G A B C

Count up 9 half steps and add any necessary accidentals.

M6

Minor seventh

given note = C♯

Go up 7 letter names and draw the top note - C D E F G A B

Count up 10 half steps and add any necessary accidentals.

m7

Major seventh

given note = B♭

Go up 7 letter names and draw the top note - B C D E F G A

Count up 11 half steps and add any necessary accidentals.

M7

HELPFUL HINTS

Notice that the major seventh is the largest interval before you get to the octave. It may be more helpful to look up the octave and then count down one half step instead of counting up eleven half steps.

Draw a minor sixth above each note.

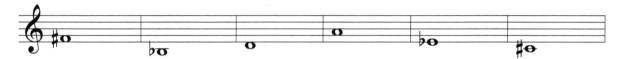

Draw a major sixth above each note.

Draw a minor seventh above each note.

Draw a major seventh above each note.

Interval	# of half steps		Interval	# of half steps
m2	1		P5	7
M2	2		m6	8
m3	3		M6	9
M3	4		m7	10
P4	5		M7	11
			P8	12

Using the chart above, identify the following intervals.

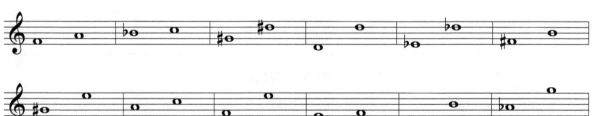

Listen to a recording of the following songs. Find and label the sixths and sevenths and then sing through each excerpt.

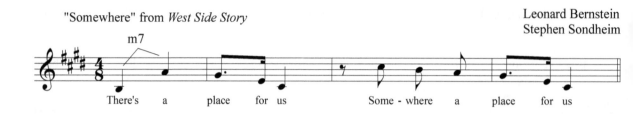

"Somewhere" from *West Side Story*   Leonard Bernstein
                                                      Stephen Sondheim

There's a place for us   Some - where a place for us

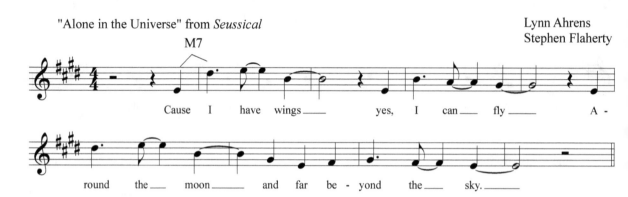

"Alone in the Universe" from *Seussical*   Lynn Ahrens
                                                      Stephen Flaherty

Cause I have wings____ yes, I can__ fly ____ A -

round the __ moon ____ and far be - yond the __ sky. _____

Additional song repertoire featuring sixths and sevenths:

"Sunday" from *Sunday in the Park with George.*
"For Good" from *Wicked.*
"Bui Doi" from *Miss Saigon.*
"Forget about the Boy" from *Thoroughly Modern Millie.*

Rests

Rests indicate silence in a piece of music. The silence is measured in the same way that we measure notes. The different types of rests parallel the different types of notes.

A whole rest—   -   = to the duration of a whole note

A half rest—   -   = to the duration of a half note

A quarter rest—   ⸯ   = to the duration of a quarter note

An eighth rest—   ⸯ   = to the duration of an eighth note

A sixteenth rest—   ⸯ   = to the duration of a sixteenth note

On the staff below, you will find rests notated. Observe that the whole rest is hanging under the "d" line while the half rest sits on the "b" line. This is how you differentiate the two rests.

whole rest   half rests   quarter rests   eighth rests   sixteenth rests
4 beats   2 beats each 1 beat each   1/2 beat each   1/4 beat each

Practice counting and clapping the following rhythms. Listen to both examples on the website.

Example 7-3

1 (2) 3 (4)   1 2 3 4   1 2 3 + 4 +   1 (+) 2 3 (4)

1 2 3 + 4   1 + 2 3 + 4   1 (2) 3 4   1 2 + 3 + 4

Example 7-4

1 2 3 (4) 1 + 2 +a 3 (+) 4   1 e +(a)2 + 3 4   1 + 2 + 3 4

1 (e) + a 2 3 (4) 1 (2) 3 + 4 + 1   2 e + 3 4 +   1 + 2 3 + 4 +

Draw bar lines so that each measure has four beats. Write the counts below the notes and then clap and count the rhythm.

Write the counts below the notes and then clap and count the rhythm.

1.

2.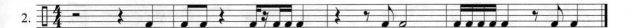

Sight-Singing

Sing the following pattern using solfege.
121314151617181 878685848382811 ***sing this every day***

Sing the following melodies using solfege while keeping a steady beat.

Listening

Listen to example 7-5 and determine if you are hearing a major or minor sixth or a major or minor seventh.

A. minor sixth	4.	11.
B. major sixth	5.	12.
C. minor seventh	6.	13.
D. major seventh	7.	14.
1.	8.	15.
2.	9.	16.
3.	10.	17.

Listen to example 7-6 and determine what interval you are hearing.

1.	7.	13.
2.	8.	14.
3.	9.	15.
4.	10.	16.
5.	11.	17.
6.	12.	18.

Listen to example 7-7 and write the RHYTHM that you hear.

Listen to example 7-8 and write the RHYTHM that you hear.

Listen to example 7-9 and write the MELODY that you hear.

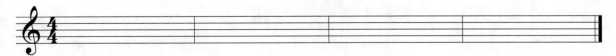

Listen to example 7-10 and write the MELODY that you hear.

8

Diminished and Augmented Intervals; Rhythm: Syncopation

Diminished and Augmented Intervals

In addition to major, minor, and perfect intervals, **diminished** and **augmented** intervals are also part of Western music. A diminished interval is a half step smaller than a perfect or minor interval. An augmented interval is a half step larger than a perfect or major interval.

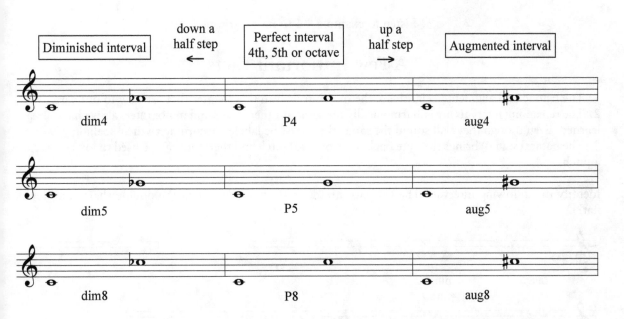

The Tritone

The augmented fourth and the diminished fifth are enharmonically the same. Both intervals are called a **tritone.** The tritone has six half steps. It comes in between the perfect fourth and perfect fifth and splits the octave in half. Be sure to count letters as well as half steps to figure out if it is an augmented fourth or a diminished fifth.

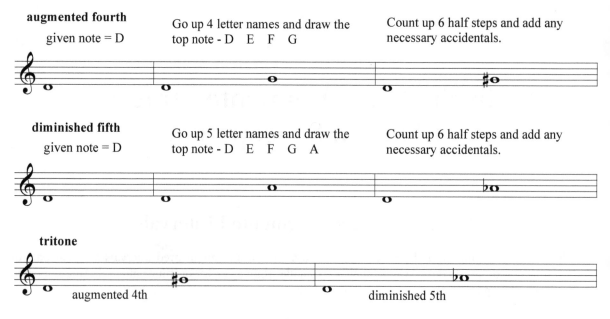

augmented fourth
given note = D

Go up 4 letter names and draw the top note - D E F G

Count up 6 half steps and add any necessary accidentals.

diminished fifth
given note = D

Go up 5 letter names and draw the top note - D E F G A

Count up 6 half steps and add any necessary accidentals.

tritone

augmented 4th   diminished 5th

Listen to example 8-1 to hear a tritone.

A Few Important Facts

1. The tritone and augmented eighth are the only intervals in this chapter that are new to our ears.
2. The remaining intervals are enharmonically the same as other major and minor intervals we have already learned. Even though they will sound the same, they must be labeled according to their spelling.
3. The **natural sign** (♮) brings the note back to its original pitch and therefore can be used to lower OR raise a pitch.

Identify the following intervals. The first two are done for you (remember the double sharp and double flat?).

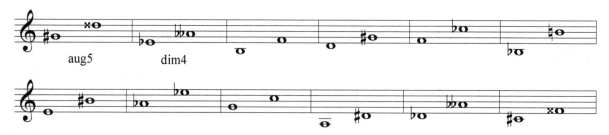

aug5   dim4

Draw a diminished fourth above each note.

Draw an augmented fourth above each note.

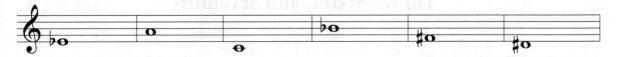

Draw a diminished fifth above each note.

Draw an augmented fifth above each note.

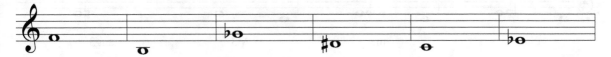

Draw a diminished eighth above each note.

Draw an augmented eighth above each note.

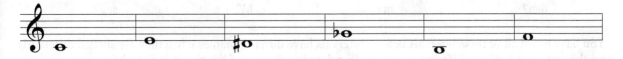

Probably the most famous example of a tritone is in "Maria" from *West Side Story*. See the excerpt below. It is written as an augmented fourth. Listen to a recording of the song to get the sound of a tritone in your ear.

Leonard Bernstein
Stephen Sondheim

"Maria" from *West Side Story*

Ma - ri - a!_____ I've just met a girl named Ma - ri - a,_____

Diminished and Augmented Seconds, Thirds, Sixths, and Sevenths

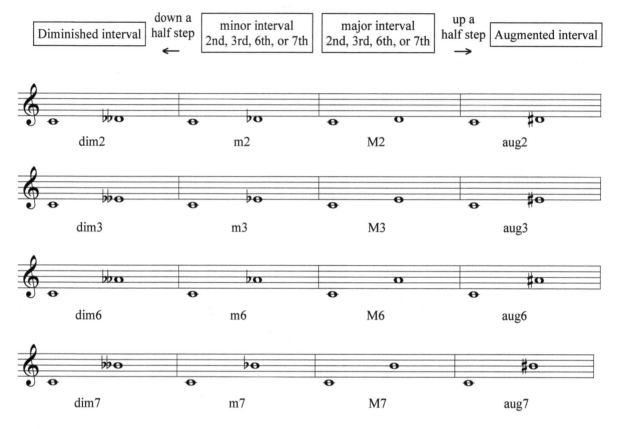

You have heard all of these intervals before. Intervals have different names when they are spelled differently on the staff. The spelling differences are usually related to the key of the music and the harmonic structure. It is not necessary to memorize the number of half steps in each of these new intervals. It is best to think of them as a half step smaller than the minor interval (diminished) or a half step larger than a major interval (augmented).

Use the chart below to aid you when working with intervals.

Interval	# of half steps
m2	1
M2	2
m3	3
M3	4
P4	5
TT	6

Interval	# of half steps
P5	7
m6	8
M6	9
m7	10
M7	11
P8	12

Identify the following intervals.

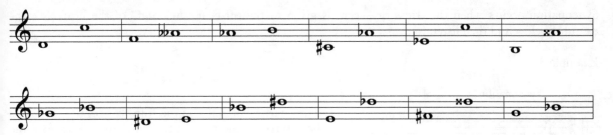

Draw the indicated interval above each note.

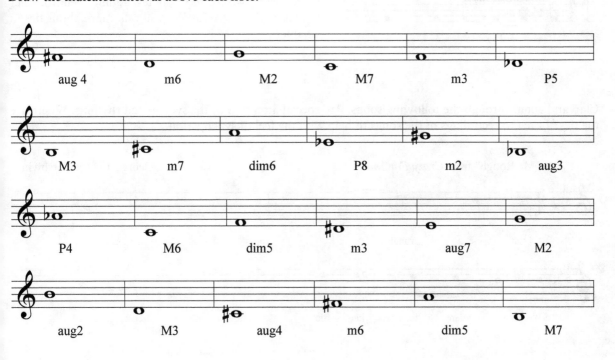

aug 4   m6   M2   M7   m3   P5

M3   m7   dim6   P8   m2   aug3

P4   M6   dim5   m3   aug7   M2

aug2   M3   aug4   m6   dim5   M7

Rhythm

Syncopation occurs when the stress or accent is given to the off-beat (the "and" of the beat). See the example below and then listen to it.

Example 8-2

The quarter note falls on the "off-beat" of beat one. It is held through the first half of beat two. Therefore the next note you hear is on the "and" of two.

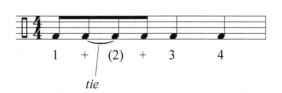

The syncopated rhythm can also be written with a **tie**. A tie connects two (or more) notes, adding them together to sound like one note. We will talk more about ties in Chapter 9.

Clap and count through the following songs. Pay special attention to the syncopated rhythms. Where are the ties? Listen to recordings of the songs to help with the feel of syncopation.

Clap and count the following rhythmic patterns. Listen to the first two examples on the website.

Example 8-3

1. 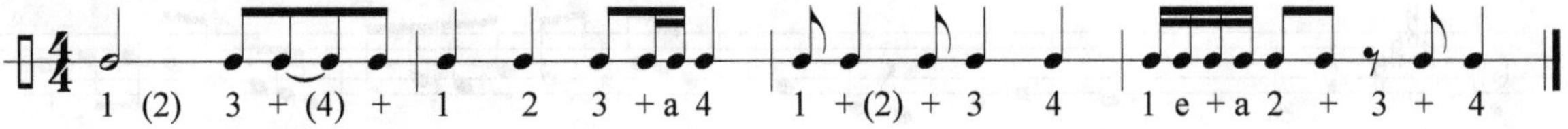 1 (2) 3 + (4) + 1 2 3 +a 4 1 +(2) + 3 4 1 e +a 2 + 3 + 4

Example 8-4

2. 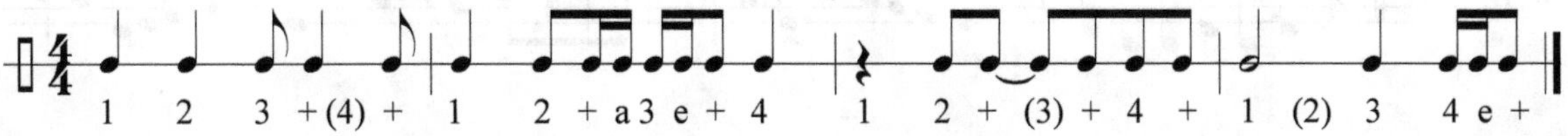 1 2 3 +(4) + 1 2 + a3 e + 4 1 2 + (3) + 4 + 1 (2) 3 4 e +

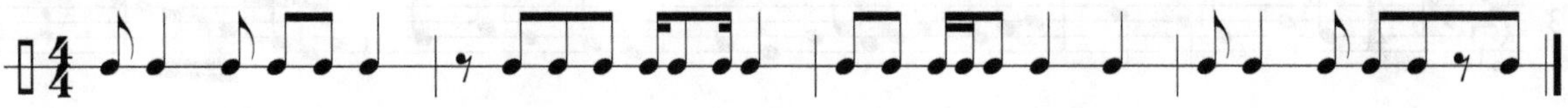

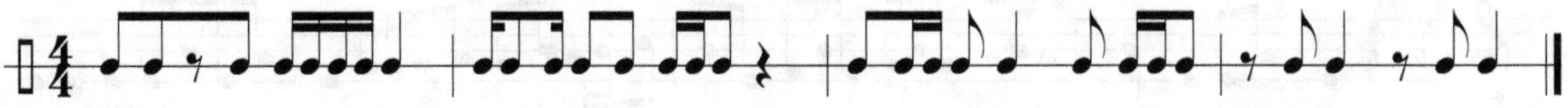

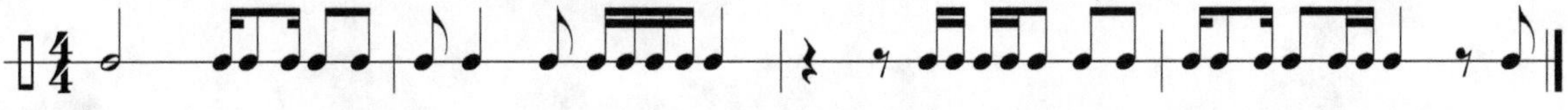

Sight-Singing

Sing the following melodies using solfege.

Listening

Remember that out of all of the augmented and diminished intervals, the only new sound is the tritone (augmented fourth or diminished fifth). Every other interval is an enharmonic spelling of an interval that we have already encountered.

Listen to example 8-5. You will hear two intervals. Determine if interval #1 or #2 is the tritone.

A. 1	4.	9.
B. 2	5.	10.
1.	6.	11.
2.	7.	12.
3.	8.	13.

Listen to example 8-6 and write the rhythm that you hear.

Listen to example 8-7 and write the rhythm that you hear.

Listen to example 8-8 and write the rhythm that you hear.

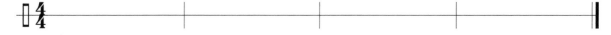

Listen to example 8-9 and write the melody that you hear.

Listen to example 8-10 and write the melody that you hear.

Listen to example 8-11 and write the melody that you hear.

Review of Chapters 5–8 and Performance Tips (Musical Markings)

Intervals

HELPFUL HINTS

1. All intervals have an inversion. There are twelve half steps in an octave. If you subtract the number of half steps in any interval from twelve, you will find the number of half steps in its inversion.

EXAMPLE: 12–5 = 7
5 half steps = a perfect fourth
7 half steps = a perfect fifth

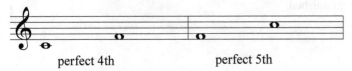

perfect 4th   perfect 5th

The notes are the same (C and F) but the interval is inverted.

EXAMPLE: 12–3 = 9
3 half steps = a minor third
9 half steps = a major sixth

minor 3rd   major 6th

The notes are the same (D and F) but the interval is inverted.

EXAMPLE: 12–6 = 6
6 half steps = a tritone

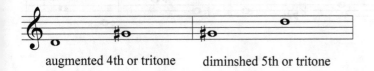

augmented 4th or tritone   diminshed 5th or tritone

The notes are the same (G# and D) but the interval is inverted. The tritone is special because it is exactly half of an octave.

2. Think about the major key signature of the bottom note of the interval. Next, see if the top note fits in that key. If it does, the interval is perfect or major.

EXAMPLES:

Think - key of D
G fits in the key

Think - key of E
G♯ fits in the key

Think - key of B♭
A fits in the key

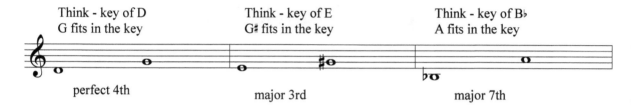

perfect 4th   major 3rd   major 7th

3. Abbreviations that are most often used:
Major interval—M: M2, M3, M7, M6
minor interval—m: m2, m3, m7, m6
Perfect interval—P: P4, P5
Tritone—TT

4. Always draw the basic interval first (third, fourth, etc.) and then add the accidentals (if necessary) to make it minor, major, perfect, augmented, or diminished.

Identify the following intervals.

Draw the following intervals.

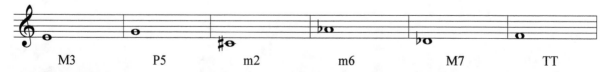

M3   P5   m2   m6   M7   TT

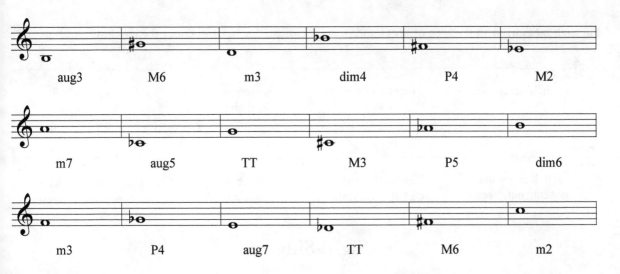

Draw the following notes and rests and indicate the number of beats they receive in 4/4 time.

whole note/rest—

half note/rest—

quarter note/rest—

eighth note/rest—

sixteenth note/rest—

Draw in the bar lines and then clap and count the rhythm.

Fill each measure with the type of notes and/or rests indicated. Clap and count the rhythm.

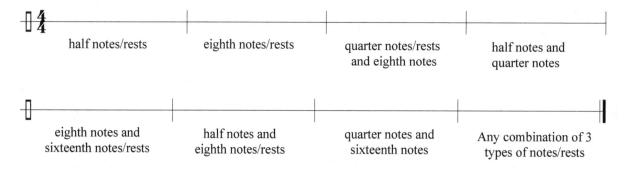

| half notes/rests | eighth notes/rests | quarter notes/rests and eighth notes | half notes and quarter notes |

| eighth notes and sixteenth notes/rests | half notes and eighth notes/rests | quarter notes and sixteenth notes | Any combination of 3 types of notes/rests |

Sight-Singing

Sing the melodies using solfege.

Listening

Listen to example R-1 and identify the interval that you hear.

1.	11.	21.
2.	12.	22.
3.	13.	23.
4.	14.	24.
5.	15.	25.
6.	16.	26.
7.	17.	27.
8.	18.	28.
9.	19.	29.
10.	20.	30.

Listen to example R-2 and write the rhythm that you hear.

Listen to example R-3 and write the rhythm that you hear.

Listen to example R-4 and write the melody that you hear.

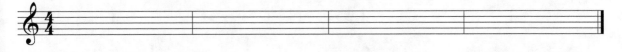

Listen to example R-5 and write the melody that you hear.

Performance Tips

Articulations are the attack and release of each note:

- — tenuto   = hold the note to its full value
- · staccato = shorten or detach the note
- > accent   = place emphasis on the note
- ⌢ fermata = sustain the note for longer than its value

Dynamics indicate the volume of the music:

pp	pianissimo	= very soft
p	piano	= soft
mp	mezzo piano	= moderately soft
mf	mezzo forte	= moderately loud
f	forte	= loud
ff	fortissimo	= very loud
subito *p*	piano	= suddenly soft
◁	crescendo	= gradually get louder
▷	decrescendo	= gradually get softer
dim.	diminuendo	= gradually get softer

9

Rhythm: Ties, Dotted Notes, 2/4 and 3/4 Time; Song Analysis

Rhythm

Tie

As we saw in Chapter 8, a tie is a curved line that connects two or more notes of the same pitch. The note values are added together and the note is held as one.

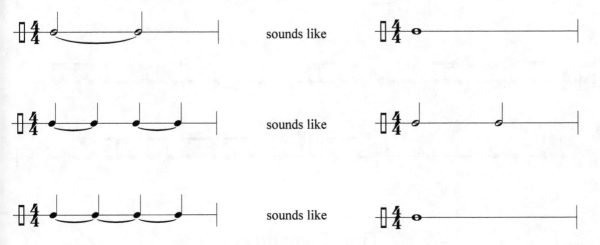

Dotted Notes

Placing a dot after a note adds half the note value to the length of that note.

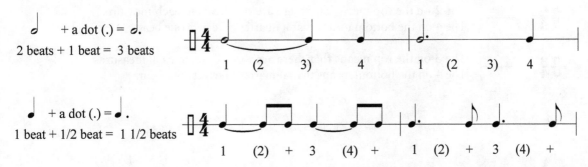

Draw in the bar lines and then count and clap the rhythm.

Time Signatures

In addition to 4/4 time, there are other time signatures that are used to group the music into measures. The time signature can give the music a different rhythmic feel.

$\frac{2}{4}$ The 2 on the top means that there are two beats in each measure.
The 4 on the bottom means that a quarter note gets one beat.

$\frac{3}{4}$ The 3 on the top means that there are three beats in each measure.
The 4 on the bottom means that a quarter note gets one beat.

The 4 on the bottom means that the note values stay the same in these new time signatures. The difference is the total number beats in each in measure.

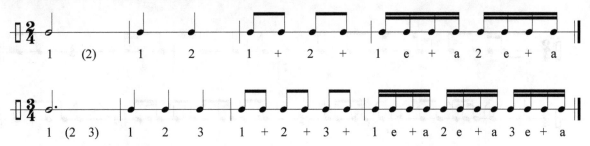

Draw in the bar lines and then count and clap the rhythm.

Clap and count the rhythm.

Sight-Singing

Sing the melodies using solfege.

Song Analysis

Now that we have determined how to perform many different rhythms, what can we learn from them? When working on a piece of music, the rhythm can give us clues about breath, articulation, style, and interpretation of the lyrics. Let's take a look at a few of the songs we have sung and learn more about them through the rhythm.

"Someday" from *The Wedding Singer*   Matthew Sklar
                                                        Chad Beguelin

How do you know when to breathe in a song? Most of the time the composer and lyricist will tell you! Look at the placement of the rests in "Someday." They are spaced at the end of each two-bar phrase right when there is a slight pause in thought. You do not have to take a breath at every rest, but the rests are the first place you should consider breathing. The next step is to consider the tempo marking. In the score, the music is marked at 136 bpm, which is relatively fast. Based on the speed, it makes more sense to breathe every four bars instead of every two bars. Lastly, consider the lyrics. If you take a breath every four bars, are the phrases set up with clear acting beats? Does the sentence structure make sense?

"Someday when it's me I'll know our love was meant to be
not one single complication or cause for hesitation" [no rest—but you can cut the half note short and take a breath]

"Someday when the dream is coming true
All you'll need is me and all I'll need is you."

In the case of this excerpt, the phrasing in the music clarifies the acting moments and gives the singer plenty of time to take each breath.

"Time Stops" from *Big Fish*   Andrew Lippa

Time stops when sud-den-ly___ you see her. Time stops and what you thought you knew

chan - ges And life be-yond this mo - ment___ is bet-ter, ___ big-ger___

Time stops, but still, your heart is beat-ing. Time stops, though you don't take a breath.

She's there and all you've e-ver want-ed is near-er,_____ clear-er._____

"Time Stops" from *Big Fish* uses rhythm in many interesting and informative ways. I am going to point out three examples, but I encourage you to look for more.

1. "Time Stops," the title of the song, is also one of the most recurring phrases. Each time we hear the phrase, the word "time" is long and on the down beat while the word "stops" is on a short up-beat followed by rests. This gives the actor insight into the importance of time as well as the feeling of a sudden stop and the silence to experience a pause in the action.

2. Look at the lyric "suddenly" in the second measure. Think about the syllabic accents of the word. The first syllable is accented. The composer/lyricist helps to emphasize that by putting that syllable on the down beat of the measure. Also, what is the meaning of "suddenly"? Often it is referring to something that quickly comes out of nowhere. Here, the word suddenly comes after the rests and is set to fast sixteenth notes. This setting further emphasizes the meaning of the word.

3. Read through the second measure of each four-bar phrase. The rhythms vary slightly based on the lyrics and number of syllables, but the basic idea of the melody is still there. In the tenth measure, the word "still" is set on a dotted eighth note. This stands out because it creates a secondary pause right after the rests. In addition, there is a comma after the word "still." The composer/lyricist is asking the actor to take a second to feel his heart still beating; maybe to wonder about it or second guess it. The interpretation can be different for each actor but the idea comes from the rhythm and the lyrics.

Listening

Listen to example 9-1 and write the rhythm that you hear.

Listen to example 9-2 and write the rhythm that you hear.

Listen to example 9-3 and write the rhythm that you hear.

Listen to example 9-4 and write the melody that you hear.

Listen to example 9-5 and write the melody that you hear.

Listen to example 9-6 and write the melody that you hear.

10

Major Triads; Introduction to Bass Clef and the Grand Staff

Major Triads

A **chord** is a grouping of three or more notes.
A **triad** is a three-note chord.

All triads are made up of two thirds stacked on top of one another. A major triad has a major third on the bottom and a minor third on the top. Listen to example 10-1 to hear a major triad.

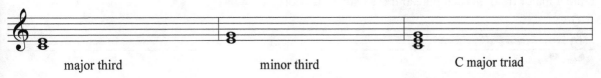

   major third   minor third   C major triad

The name of the triad is the **root** of the chord (the bottom note that you build the chord on).

Each triad must be made up of three "line" notes or three "space" notes. It is helpful to draw the three notes first (a snowman) and then figure out what accidentals are necessary to create the proper thirds.

Use the keyboard to help visualize each triad.

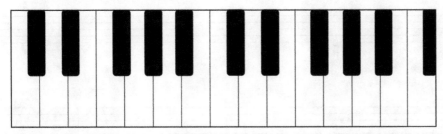

Remember, a major triad has a major third on the bottom and a minor third on the top.

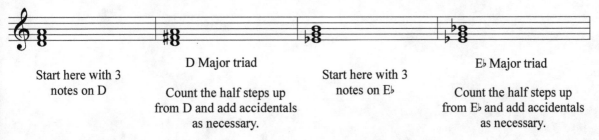

           D Major triad   E♭ Major triad

Start here with 3   Start here with 3
notes on D   notes on E♭

       Count the half steps up   Count the half steps up
       from D and add accidentals   from E♭ and add accidentals
         as necessary.   as necessary.

You can also think of building a major triad by using a major scale. You can take any major scale and stack do, mi, and sol (1, 3, and 5) to get a major triad.

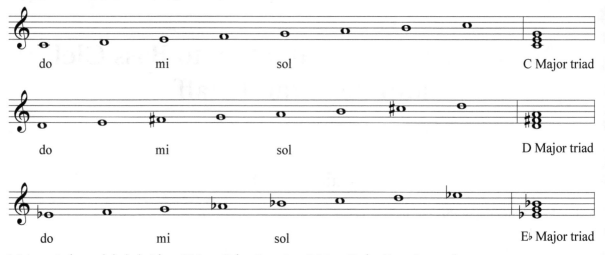

Major triads are labeled either CM or C for C major; DM or D for D major, and so on.

Build a major triad on each note and then label the chord below.

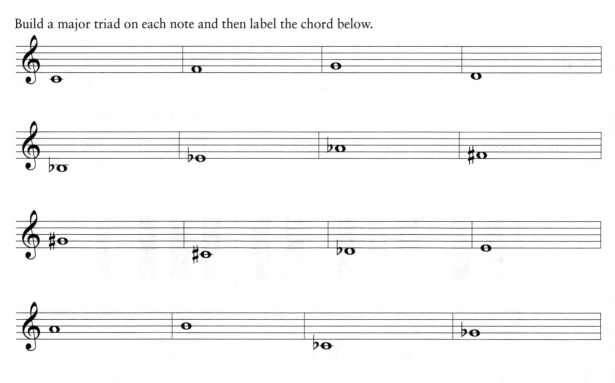

Bass Cleff

The bass clef (also known as the F clef) is used for lower instruments and voices. Practice drawing the bass clef below

When using bass clef, the pitches of the lines and spaces are as follows.

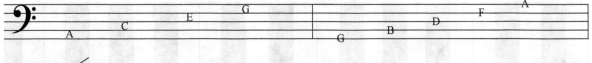

 Notice that the F is on the fourth line, which is surrounded by the two dots of the bass clef. That is why this clef is also called the F clef.

Identify the following notes.

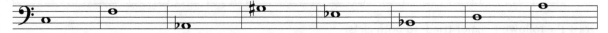

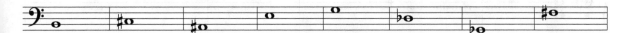

Draw the following notes.

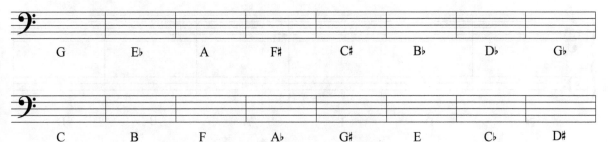

| G | E♭ | A | F♯ | C♯ | B♭ | D♭ | G♭ |

| C | B | F | A♭ | G♯ | E | C♭ | D♯ |

The Grand Staff

The treble clef and bass clef can be joined together by a brace. This is called the grand staff. It is used mainly in piano music.

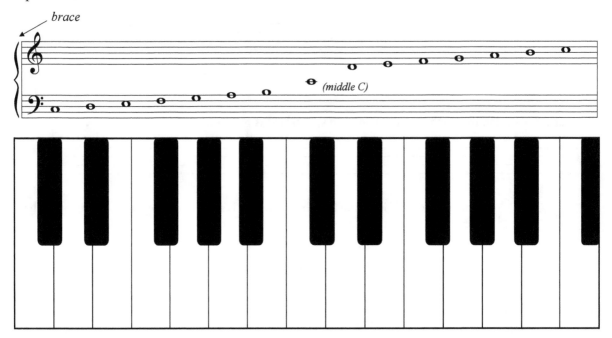

Draw the following major triads in both clefs.

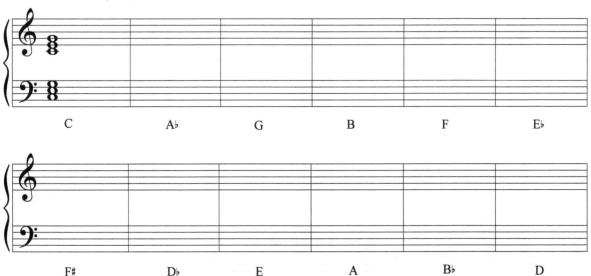

Sight-Singing

Sing the following melodies using solfege.

Listening

Listen to example 10-2 and write the melody you hear.

Listen to example 10-3 and write the melody you hear.

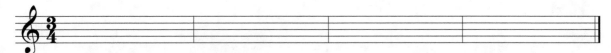

Listen to example 10-4 and write the melody you hear.

Rewrite 10-2 in bass clef.

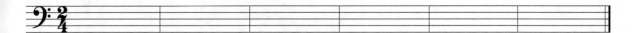

Rewrite 10-3 in bass clef.

Rewrite 10-4 in bass clef.

11

I, IV, V Progression; Chord Tones and Non-Chord Tones; Song Analysis

In each major key you will find three major triads. These triads are built on the first, fourth, and fifth notes of the major scale. You do not need to add any accidentals to the chords since they already appear in the key signature. The chords are labeled with Roman numerals below and chord names above.

Draw the following scales and I, IV, and V chords. Label each chord with both the chord name and Roman numeral. Don't forget to draw the key signature first.

F#:

D♭:

Draw the I, IV, and V chords in each key. Label each chord with both the chord name and the Roman numeral. Watch out for clef changes!

F:

A:

B:

E♭:

G:

C#:

D:

G♭:

The I, IV, V progression is found in all styles of musical theatre. Here are a few examples.

*The accompaniment has been altered to simplify the analysis.

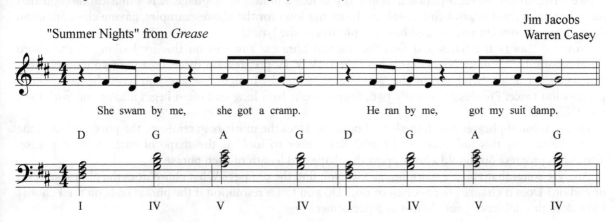

"Summer Nights" from *Grease*

Jim Jacobs
Warren Casey

"Leavin's Not the Only Way To Go" from *Big River*

Roger Miller

"Comedy Tonight" from *A Funny Thing Happened On The Way To The Forum*

Stephen Sondheim

Song Analysis

As we have already noted, a **phrase** in music is just like a phrase in language. It is a musical thought that has a beginning, middle, and end. Speak the lyrics out loud for the above examples, paying close attention to the punctuation. Do you see and hear the phrases of the lyrics?

Now take away the lyrics and find the musical phrases. You can do this by looking at the chord progressions. In "Summer Nights" you have the I, IV, V, IV progression twice, creating two mini phrases. The same is true of "Children of the Wind" and "Comedy Tonight," where you have the same chord progression twice. Phrases are usually two, four or eight bars long and often begin and/or end with the I and V chords.

Do the musical phrases match the lyrical phrases? Does the music help reinforce the punctuation in the lyrics? How does this influence the breath? Remember to look at the shape of each melodic phrase. The chord progression should also support the shape and length of each phrase.

Analyze songs that you are working on. Can you find the phrases? What chord does the phrase start on or end on? Does it change chords often or not? Do you feel a resolution if the phrase ends on the I chord? How does this influence your choices as a performer?

Chord Tones *and* Non-Chord Tones

Chord tones are notes that are found in the chord.
Non-chord tones are notes that are not found in the chord.
* Non-chord tones are prevalent in musical theatre repertoire. They create colors and dissonances that can make phrases more interesting and help further the storytelling. As you learn more about harmony, you will find that almost every note is related in some way.

The arrows point to the non-chord tones in the following melody. These are notes that are not in the chord that is being played below the melody line. Play the chords on the piano and sing the melody line. What do you hear?

Circle the non-chord tones in the melody. Play the chords on the piano and sing the melody.

You can harmonize a melody by analyzing the notes. In this exercise, the majority of the notes in each measure are usually chord tones. Using the I, IV, and V chords in the key of E♭ major, harmonize the following melody and then circle the non-chord tones. You may want to list the notes in the three chords as a reference. You should find one chord per measure. Label the chords with Roman numerals below the staff and chord names above the staff.

Harmonize the following melodies using the I, IV, and V chords found in each key. There may be more than one chord per measure. Watch the "labeling lines" below the staff as a guide. Circle the non-chord tones and label the chords (Roman numerals below the staff and chord names above the staff).

2.

Using a combination of chord tones and non-chord tones, write a melody to go with the chords below. Label the chords and circle the non-chord tones. Sing the melody using solfege.

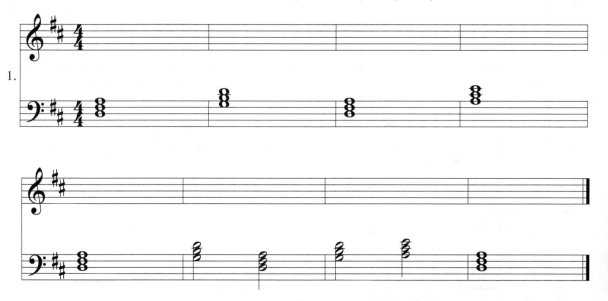

1.

2.

12

Transpositions; Rhythm: Triplets

Transposition

Transposition is the process of moving a pitch or collection of pitches up or down by a set interval while keeping the relationship of the pitches constant. Musicians, especially singers, can transpose songs into keys that work best for their instrument. You can think of transposition in two ways: by intervals or by key relationship.

Transposing by Interval

Move each pitch up or down by the prescribed interval.

Original melody:

Transpose the melody up a major third.

Each pitch is raised a major third. Use your keyboard to check each interval.

Raise the original melody up a perfect fifth.

Lower the original melody by a whole step.

Raise the original melody by a half step.

Lower the original melody by a minor third.

Notice that the relationship between the pitches in the melody stays constant. For example, the distance from the first note to second note is always a whole step. The distance from the third note to the fourth note is always a minor third.

Transposing by Key

You have been transposing by key since Chapter 4 when you started sight-singing with solfege. Solfege keeps the relationship between the pitches constant no matter what key you are in.

Original melody in the key of C:

sol   mi re mi   la   do   re   sol   fa   do re mi sol la   mi   sol   do

Transpose the melody up a perfect fourth into the key of F using solfege.

sol   mi re mi   la   do   re   sol   fa   do re mi sol la   mi   sol   do

Transpose the melody up a minor third into the key of E♭ using solfege.

Transpose the melody down a half step into the key of B using solfege.

Transpose the melody down a minor third into the key of A using solfege.

Transpose the melody up a whole step into the key of D♭ using solfege.

When transposing chords, use Roman numeral analysis to move the chords to any key.
Original melody and chords in the key of D:

sol mi sol la do   ti   la   fa mi do re   mi   sol do re do ti sol   do   re   do

Transpose the melody and chords into the key of F major.

Transpose the melody and chords into the key of A♭ major.

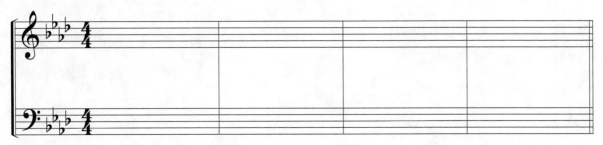

Transpose the melody and chords into the key of B major.

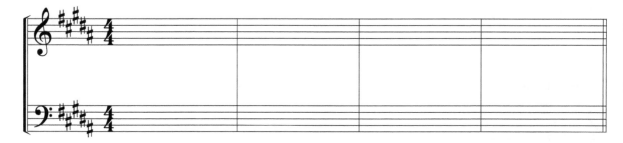

Triplets

Triplets consist of three notes of equal value that fit into a specified amount of time. An eighth note triplet consists of three eighth notes that fill one beat. Each eighth note in the triplet is equal in length and receives a third of a beat.

Clap and count the following examples and then listen to them on the website.

Example 12-1

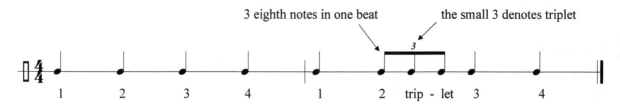

Example 12-2

Example 12-3

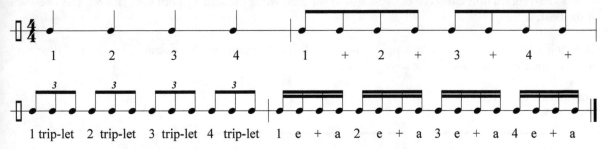

Triplets may also contain rests.

a bracket is used when the notes and rests
are not connected by a beam

Example 12-4

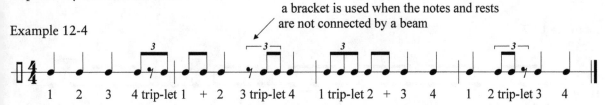

Example 12-5

Clap and count the following rhythmic patterns. Use a metronome to help keep a steady beat.

Eighth note triplets can also be made up of one quarter note and one eighth note. Since a quarter note is equal to two eighth notes, it receives two-thirds of the beat while the single eighth note still receives one-third of the beat.

Clap and count the following examples and then listen to them on the website. The first and second measure should sound exactly the same.

Example 12-6

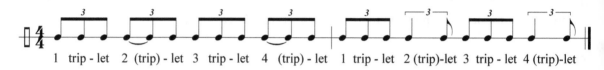

1 trip - let   2 (trip) - let   3 trip - let   4 (trip) - let   1 trip - let   2 (trip)-let   3 trip - let   4 (trip)-let

Example 12-7

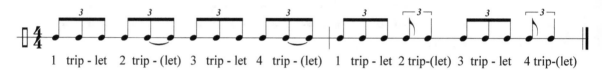

1 trip - let   2 trip - (let)   3 trip - let   4 trip - (let)   1 trip - let   2 trip-(let)   3 trip - let   4 trip-(let)

Clap and count the following examples. Use a metronome to help keep a steady beat.

Clap and count through the following song examples and then listen to a recording.

"What Did I Have That I Don't Have?"   Alan Jay Lerner
from *On a Clear Day You Can See Forever*   Burton Lane

What is-n't there that once was there?   What have I got   a great big lack of?

Some-thing in me then   he could see then   beck-ons to him no   more.

"Happy to Keep His Dinner Warm"   Frank Loesser
from *How To Succeed in Business Without Really Trying*

I'll be so   hap-py to keep his din-ner warm____while he goes   on-ward___   and   up-ward.___

Hap-py to keep hi din-ner warm_____   till   he comes wear-i-ly home   from down

A quarter note triplet consists of three quarter notes that fill two beats. Each quarter note in the triplet is equal and receives two-thirds of a beat. The quarter note triplet feels a bit like syncopation since the second and third notes are just off the beat. Compare lines 1 and 2 to see how the triplets line up.

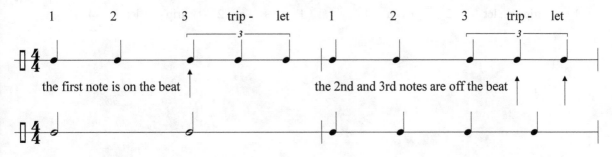

1   2   3   trip -   let   1   2   3   trip -   let

the first note is on the beat   the 2nd and 3rd notes are off the beat

Clap and count the following examples and then listen to them on the website.

Example 12-8

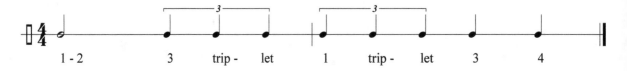

Example 12-9

Example 12-10

Example 12-11

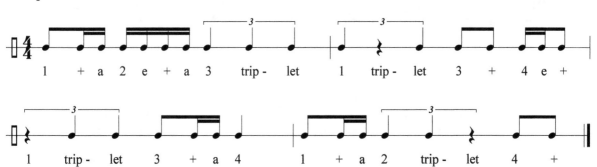

Clap and count through the following song example and then listen to a recording.

"Good Morning Baltimore" from *Hairspray*

Marc Shaiman
Scott Wittman

Clap and count the following rhythmic patterns. Use a metronome to help keep a steady beat.

Review of Chapters 9–12 and Performance Tips (Repeats, Endings, and Codas)

Major Triads

We learned how to draw major triads two different ways. One way is by stacking thirds and the other is working within a major key signature. Follow the directions below to reinforce the process for both methods.

Drawing a Major Triad by Stacking Thirds: The "Snowman" Method

1. Start by drawing the root of the chord.

*For an E major triad, start by drawing the E

2. Draw a snowman on top of the bottom note.

3. On a keyboard, count up four half steps from the bottom note to the middle note. What note do you end on? Is that what you have drawn? Do you need to add an accidental?

*Here we need to add a sharp to make the middle note G♯.

4. On a keyboard, count up three half steps from the middle note to the top note. What note do you end on? Is that what you have drawn? Do you need to add an accidental?

*Here we end on B and do not need to add an accidental.

HELPFUL HINTS

1. Make sure you draw the correct starting note: A D♭ chord has to start with a D♭ on the bottom (not a D).
2. Make sure you draw the snowman before counting the half steps.
3. Remember that a half step is the *distance* between each note—you aren't counting the notes themselves.

Draw the indicated major triads in both the treble clef and bass clef. Use the snowman method.

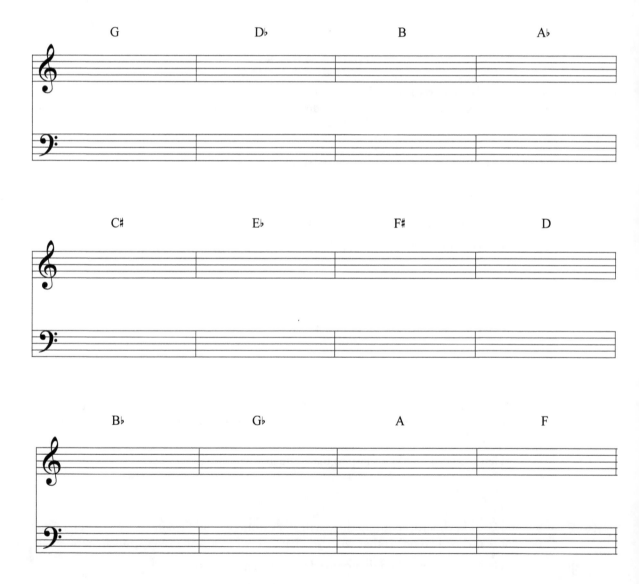

Drawing Major Triads in a Major Key

The I, IV, and V chords in a major key are all major.

1. Draw the key signature first.

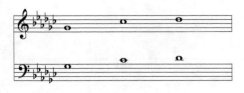

2. Draw the first, fourth and fifth notes of the scale.

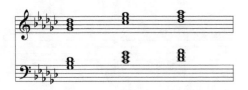

3. Draw a snowman on top of each note.

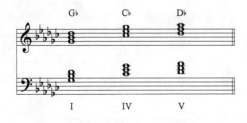

4. Label the chords using chord names above and Roman numerals below.

HELPFUL HINTS

1. Make sure you double check your key signature.
2. Remember you don't have to add any accidentals to the chords. The flats and sharps in the key signature do the work for you.
3. When naming the chords, don't forget to write flats and sharps in the name of the chord (if necessary).
4. Only the I, IV, and V chords in a major key are major. Chords starting on other scale degrees are not major chords.

Draw the major key signature and then draw the I, IV, and V chords in that key. Label the chords with chord names and Roman numerals.

A Major:

Bb Major:

Db Major:

F Major:

E Major:

G Major:

Rhythm Practice

Draw in the missing bar lines and then clap and count the exercise.

Clap and count the following exercises.

Performance Tips

The Road Map

Repeat signs, first and second endings, codas etc. How do I find my way around?

Some songs are simple: you start at the beginning and then continue singing/playing straight through until you get to the final measure. In other cases you will find markings in your music to repeat certain sections or skip a section. This can save paper and ink but can take some time to figure out.

Repeat Signs

When you get to the backwards repeat sign, you go back to the forward repeat sign and start again. Often you will see this with the word **vamp** over it. In musical theatre, a vamp is mostly used under dialogue. The orchestra will continue to repeat the vamp until the singer(s) are ready to begin singing.

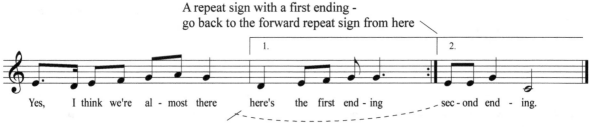

The slash with a dot on either side (✗) is also a repeat sign (a **one-bar repeat**). It means to repeat the bar directly before it and then go on. This notation is seen mainly in instrumental parts (especially percussion parts).

The Road Map (Continued)

D.C.	Da capo (from the beginning)
Fine	The end
D.C. al fine	Back to the beginning until "fine"
⊕ Coda	The concluding passage of a piece of music
D.C. al Coda	Back to the beginning and then to the Coda
To Coda	To the Coda

This is the end (the 2nd time around)

Fine

D.C. al Fine

Here you go back to the begining

D.S.	Dal Segno (from the sign)
D.S. al fine	Back to the sign until "fine"
D.S. al Coda	Back to the sign and then to the Coda
𝄋	the sign

𝄋 (the sign)

Go to the Coda the 2nd time

To Coda

Go back to the sign

D.S. al Coda

⊕ the Coda

13

Minor, Diminished, and Augmented Triads; Cut-Time; Chromatic Solfege

Minor Triads

As we discussed in Chapter 10, all triads are made up of two thirds stacked on top of one another. A **minor triad** has a minor third on the bottom and a major third on the top. The outer interval (from the bottom note to the top note) is a perfect fifth. Listen to example 13-1 to hear a minor triad.

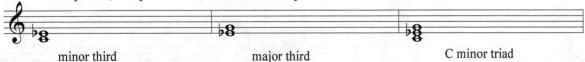

minor third   major third   C minor triad

The name of the triad is the root of the chord (the bottom note that you build the chord on). Each triad must be made up of three "line" notes or three "space" notes. It is helpful to draw the three notes first and then figure out what accidentals are necessary to create the proper thirds.

Use the keyboard to help visualize each triad.

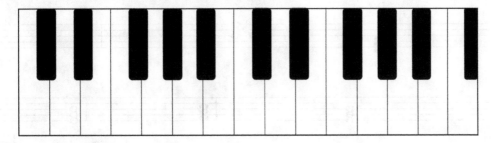

Remember, a minor triad has a minor third on the bottom and a major third on the top.

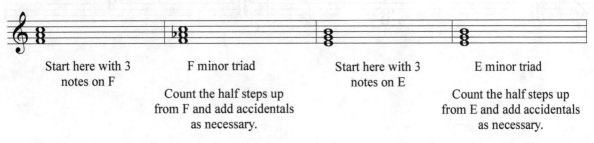

Start here with 3   F minor triad   Start here with 3   E minor triad
notes on F   notes on E

Count the half steps up   Count the half steps up
from F and add accidentals   from E and add accidentals
as necessary.   as necessary.

Minor triads are labeled either C- or Cm for C minor; D- or Dm for D minor, and so on.

Build a minor triad on each note and then label the chord below.

Label the following chords. But be careful—some are minor and some are major.

Listening

1. Listen to example 13-2. You will hear a number of minor chords.
2. Listen to example 13-3. Identify each chord as either major or minor.

1. M	2. m	3.	4.	5.	6.	7.	8.	9.	10.
11.	12.	13.	14.	15.	16.	17.	18.	19.	20.

Diminished Triads

A diminished triad is made up of <u>two minor thirds.</u>

      minor third   minor third   C diminished triad

*Notice that the outer interval (from the bottom note to the top note) is a diminished fifth unlike major and minor triads.

Diminished triads are labeled either C° or C dim for C diminished, D° or D dim for D diminished, and so on.

Build a diminished triad on each note and then label the chord below and listen to example 13-4.

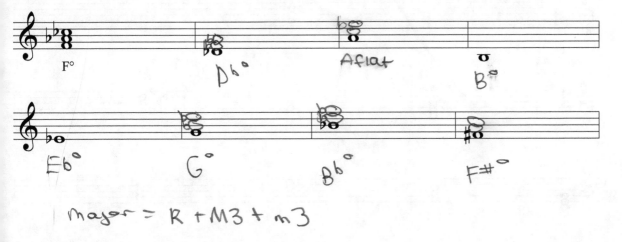

F°   D♭°   A flat   B°

E♭°   G°   B♭°   F♯°

major = R + M3 + m3

Augmented Triads

An augmented triad is made up of two major thirds.

major third   major third   C augmented triad

*Notice that the outer interval is an augmented fifth.

Augmented triads are labeled either C+ or C aug for C augmented, D+ or D aug for D augmented, and so on.

Build an augmented triad on each note and label the chord below and listen to example 13-5.

E+

Analyze the following chords and label them (major, minor, diminished, or augmented).

F#°   E-

Listening

Listen to example 13-6. You will hear a number of diminished chords.

Listen to example 13-7. You will hear a number of augmented chords.

Listen to example 13-8. Identify each chord as either, major, minor, diminished, or augmented.

1.	8.	15.	22.
2.	9.	16.	23.
3.	10.	17.	24.
4.	11.	18.	25.
5.	12.	19.	26.
6.	13.	20.	27.
7.	14.	21.	28.

Cut-Time

In addition to 4/4, 3/4, and 2/4 time, we have other time signatures where the quarter note is not equal to one beat. It is important to note, however, that the relationship between the notes stays the same (i.e. two half notes are equal to one whole note which is equal to four quarter notes).

The 2 on the top means that there are two beats in each measure.
The 2 on the bottom means that a half note gets one beat.

You will often see 2/2 time or cut-time written this way instead of with the 2/2. They mean the same thing and are interchangeable.

Music written in cut-time often looks the same as music written in 4/4 time. The difference is usually in the speed (beats per minute—bpm) and the feel or accent of the music.

Count and clap the following exercise in 4/4 time. Set your metronome to 120 bpm.

Example 13-9

Now count and clap the same exercise in cut-time. Set your metronome to 70 bpm. Remember that the half note is equal to one beat.

Example 13-10

Can you feel a difference between the 4/4 version and the cut-time version? Pay attention to the accents that you feel with each half note pulse. Clap and count that following examples in the same way.

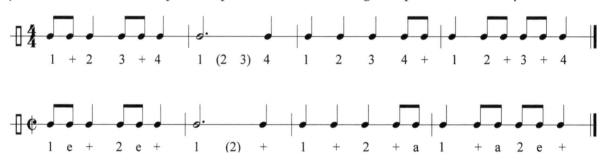

Clap and count the following song excerpts and then listen to a recording. Notice that "Popular" starts in 4/4 time and then switches to cut time. How does that affect what she is saying?

Also, notice there are notes with added accidentals in both excerpts. For these notes, we use **chromatic solfege.**

"Popular" from *Wicked*   Stephen Schwartz

And e-ven in your case, though it's the tough-est case I've yet to face, ___ don't

wor-ry, I'm de-ter-minied to suc-ceed, Fol-low my lead and yes, in-deed you will be

Pop - u - lar. ___ You're gon - na be pop-u - lar! I'll teach you the

pro - per ploys when you talk to boys, lit - tle ways to flirt and flounce, ___ (ooh!)

Clap and count the following exercises. Use a metronome to help keep a steady beat.

14

I, vi, ii, V, I Progression; Harmonizing a Melody

As we discussed in Chapter 11, you can build a major chord on the first, fourth, and fifth scale degrees in every major key.

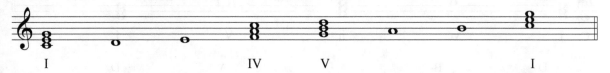

In addition to the major chords, the triads built on the second, third, and sixth scale degrees are minor chords.

The triad built on the seventh scale degree (leading tone) is a diminished chord

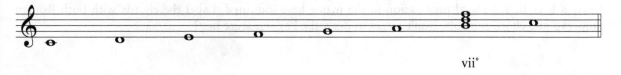

Every major key has the same set of triads.

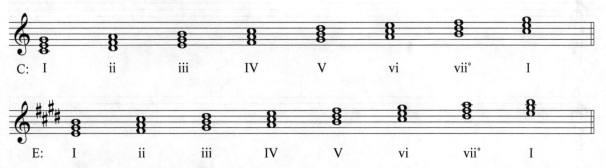

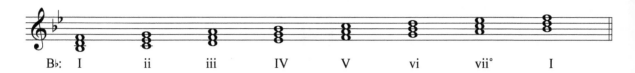

Bb: I   ii   iii   IV   V   vi   vii°   I

> Notice that the Roman numerals used for the minor and diminished triads are lower case while the Roman numerals used for major chords are upper case. This is necessary to distinguish between the different types of chords.

In addition to the I, IV, V, I progression, another common chord progression is I, vi, ii, V, I.

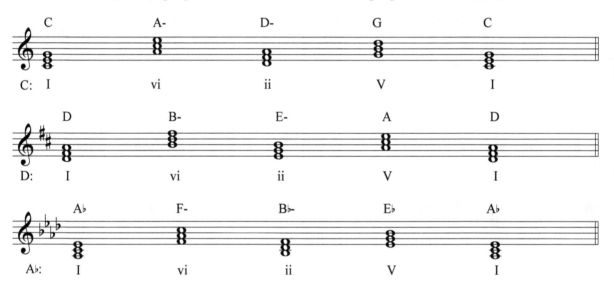

Draw a I, vi, ii, V, I chord progression in the major keys indicated. Label the chords with both Roman numerals and chord symbols. Don't forget to draw the key signature first!

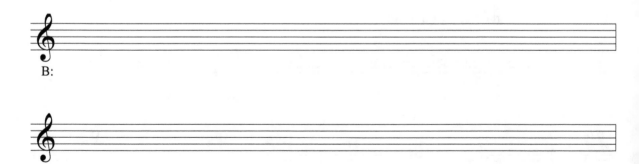

B:

Eb:

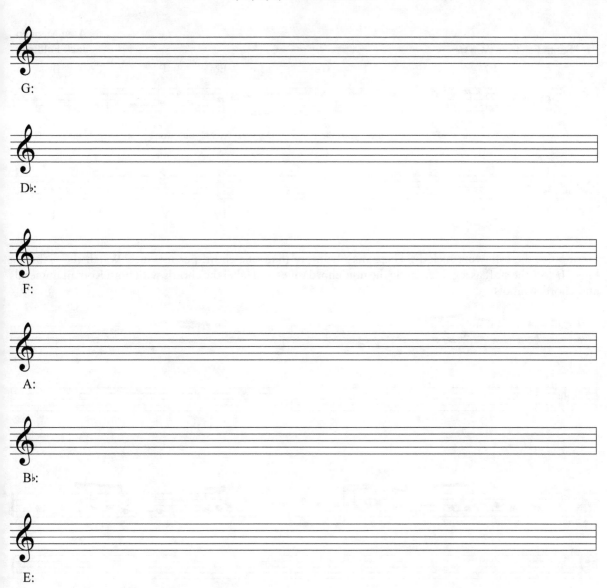

G:

Db:

F:

A:

Bb:

E:

The I, vi, ii, V progression is found in many songs. Listen to the following examples.

"It Only Takes a Moment" from *Hello, Dolly!*   Jerry Herman

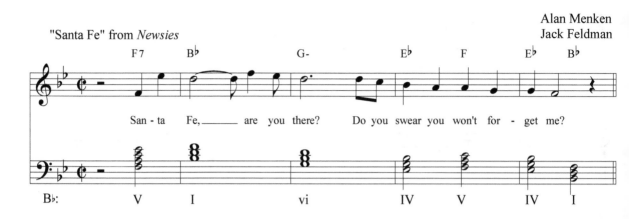

Harmonize the following melody. There may be more than one chord per measure. Watch the "labeling lines" below the staff as a guide. Circle the non-chord tones and label the chords with both Roman numerals and chord symbols.

Using a combination of chord tones and non-chord tones, write a melody to go with the following chord progression. Label the chords and circle the non-chord tones. Sing the melody using solfege.

Sing the following melodies using solfege.

15

Inversions of Triads

So far, we have worked on building chords in root position—meaning that the note that is on the bottom of the chord is the name of the chord (or root). You will also find chords written in inversions. This facilitates smooth voice leading and gives the musician more opportunities to create slightly different colors with the same chord. All triads have a root position as well as a first inversion and a second inversion. See below:

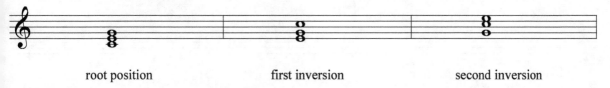

root position   first inversion   second inversion

The three notes in the C major chord are always C, E, and G, but their positions within the chord structure change.

Look at the D major chord below and its inversions.

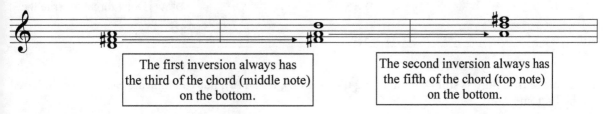

> The first inversion always has the third of the chord (middle note) on the bottom.

> The second inversion always has the fifth of the chord (top note) on the bottom.

Listen to example 15-1 to hear the D major chord played in root position and both inversions.

Draw the following chords in root position, first inversion, and second inversion. Remember to keep the accidentals the same in each chord. The notes do not change; only the order changes.

E♭ Major

B Major

C♯ Major

F Major

A Major

When working with chords in inversions, the chord symbol must indicate the inversion. We do this by writing the name of the chord first and then a slash and the bottom note of the chord. See the examples below:

The name of the chord is still D♭ (containing the notes D♭, F, and A♭), but you indicate each inversion based on the bottom note.

Draw each chord in root position, first inversion, and second inversion. Label each chord above the staff as demonstrated in the examples above.

G Major

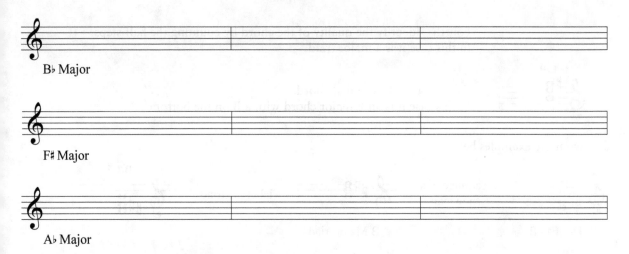

Bb Major

F# Major

Ab Major

Draw the following major chords in first inversion and label them appropriately. If necessary, draw the chord in root position first and then figure out the inversion.

Ab   B   F   E   Gb   D

Draw the following major chords in second inversion and label them appropriately. If necessary, draw the chord in root position first and then figure out the inversion.

G   Db   C   F#   A   Bb

When you are looking at a chord in an inversion, how do you know what chord it is? To figure out what triad you are looking at, rearrange the three notes of the triad on the staff until you make a snowman. That is root position. From there you can tell what the root of the triad is and whether not it is major, minor, diminished, or augmented.

For now, we will stick with major triads. Take a look at the example below.

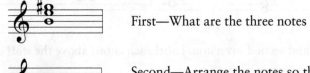

First—What are the three notes in the triad?   B—E—G#

Second—Arrange the notes so that they make a snowman on the staff (three line notes or three space notes stacked up on the staff)

Third—What is the bottom note? That is the root (name) of the chord. In this case it is E.

Fourth—Identify the quality of the chord by counting the half steps.
In this case it is a major triad.

Fifth—Label the original chord.
In this case it is an E major chord with a B on the bottom.

See two more examples below.

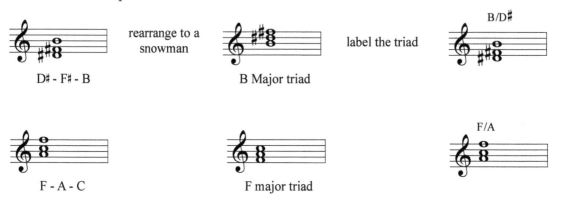

rearrange to a snowman

D♯ - F♯ - B

label the triad

B Major triad

B/D♯

F - A - C

F major triad

F/A

Identify and label the following chords.

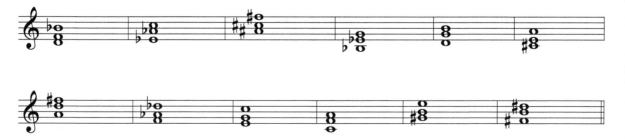

Minor, diminished, and augmented triads can be inverted in the same way.

D-   D-/F   D-/A   E°   E°/G   E°/B♭

Draw each chord in root position, first inversion, and second inversion. Label each chord above the staff as demonstrated in the examples above.

F minor

C augmented

G diminished

Draw the following chords in first inversion and label them appropriately. If necessary, draw the chord in root position first and then figure out the inversion.

F-   A   G°   E♭-   B°   D+

Draw the following chords in second inversion and label them appropriately. If necessary, draw the chord in root position first and then figure out the inversion.

E°   B♭+   F#-   D♭   C+   G♭-

Identify the following chords using the appropriate chord symbols.

Rhythm

Clap and count the rhythm.

Sight-Singing

Sing the following melodies using solfege while keeping a steady beat.

Listening

Listen to example 15-2 and write the rhythm that you hear.

Listen to example 15-3 and write the rhythm that you hear.

Listen to example 15-4 and write the melody that you hear.

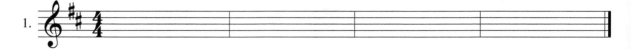

Listen to example 15-5 and write the melody that you hear.

16

Chord Progressions with Inversions

As we discussed in Chapter 11, each chord in a key can be identified with a Roman numeral. The Roman numeral assigned to a chord depends on its placement in the key and quality (major, minor, or diminished).

In the key of C major we have:

When an inversion of a chord is used, it must be represented in the Roman numeral analysis as well.

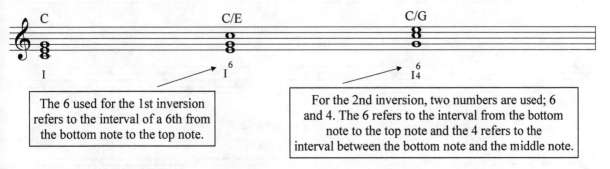

The 6 used for the 1st inversion refers to the interval of a 6th from the bottom note to the top note.

For the 2nd inversion, two numbers are used; 6 and 4. The 6 refers to the interval from the bottom note to the top note and the 4 refers to the interval between the bottom note and the middle note.

The numbers that identify the inversion are the same for every chord.

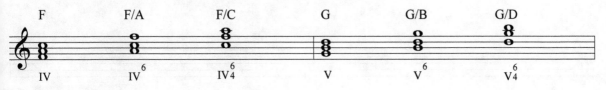

Using inversions, we can create smooth voice leading for chord progressions in any key.

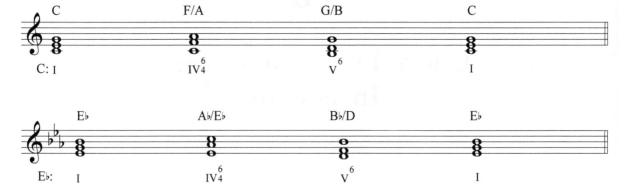

Draw a I, IV, V, I progression using smooth voice leading in the following keys. Label each chord with the appropriate Roman numeral below and chord symbol above. Don't forget to draw the key signature first.

F:

A♭:

C♯:

You can create smooth voice leading for any chord progression. Here is an example for the I, vi, ii, V, I progression. Notice how some notes stay the same from one chord to the next and others move only by a second or a third. Smooth voice leading creates even lines for each voice part in vocal/choral pieces. It also gives a pianist an easy and unbroken way to move from one chord to the next. Smooth voice leading is not always necessary or desirable. There are times where the music calls for a more disjointed or jumpy sound.

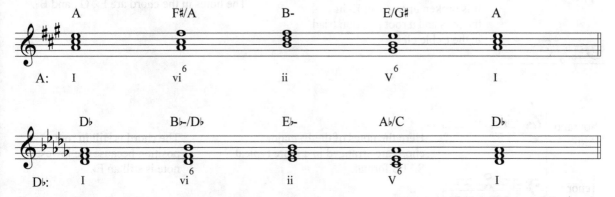

Draw a I, vi, ii, V, I progression using smooth voice leading in the following keys. Label each chord with the appropriate Roman numeral below and chord symbol above. Don't forget to draw the key signature first.

E♭:

G:

In music, the chords will often be broken up between two clefs or more. You have probably noticed this in the vocal parts of group numbers as well as in piano music. Let's look at some four-part vocal selections to analyze the chords and examine smooth voice leading.

Here we have an E♭ major chord -
It is broken up with an E♭ in
the bass and a root position triad
in the treble clef.

The notes in the chord are E♭, G , and B♭.

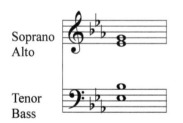

Here the notes of the E♭ major
chord are arranged in a more typical
SATB format.

The chord is still in root
position because the lowest
note is still an E♭.

It is important to remember that the inversion is based on the *lowest* note (bass note). The voicing of the upper notes can vary without affecting the inversion.

Take a look at these examples of an E♭ major chord.

In each example, the notes of the chord stay the same—E♭, G, B♭—but the note that is doubled changes. The doubled note does not alter the name of the chord although it can change the sound of the chord.

Here is a progression that is arranged in a four-part choral style. Take a look at the analysis and sing through each part. Notice how each individual voice part moves mainly by stepwise motion.

Analyze the chords with chord symbols above the staff and Roman numerals below. Sing through each exercise with a group if possible.

HELPFUL HINTS

1. Figure out the key signature and then write out all of the chords in that key (the first one is done for you).
2. Using extra staff paper, take the collection of pitches for each chord and make a snowman to figure out the name of the chord
3. Write the chord symbols first and then the Roman numerals. Once you know the names of the chords, it is much easier to figure out the corresponding Roman numeral.

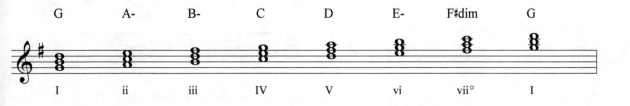

Analyze the chords with chord symbols above the staff and Roman numerals below. Sing through each song with a group if possible.

"On My Way" from *Violet*

Jeanine Tesori
Brian Crawley

*In the score for "On My Way," the tenor and baritone parts are written in treble clef but sung one octave lower.

Review of Chapters 13–16 and Performance Tips (The Music Department)

Triad Formulas

Major triad: M3, m3   Augmented triad: M3, M3
Minor triad: m3, M3   Diminished triad: m3, m3

Remember to start with the root of the triad, then build a snowman, and then count the half steps to follow the formula for each triad.

Db major triad

root note   build a snowman

m3 on top (3 half steps)

M3 on bottom (4 half steps)

F minor triad

root note   build a snowman

M3 on top (4 half steps)

m3 on bottom (3 half steps)

C diminished triad

root note   build a snowman

m3 on top (3 half steps)

m3 on bottom (3 half steps)

D augmented triad

root note   build a snowman

M3 on top (4 half steps)

M3 on bottom (4 half steps)

Draw the indicated triad.

A   G+   B-   E°

Bb+   D°   F#   C-

Eb°   F-   Db+   Ab

C#   B+   Gb°   Eb-

Label each triad.

Writing the I, vi, ii V, I progression in a major key.

A Major

1. Draw the key signature first.

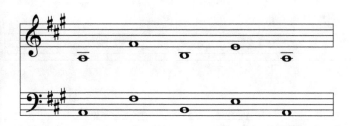

2. Draw the first, sixth, second, fifth, and first notes of the scale.

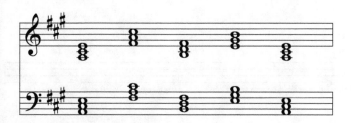

3. Draw a snowman on top of each note.

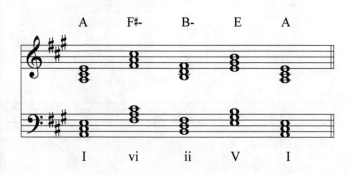

4. Label the chords using chord names above and Roman numerals below.

Draw a I, vi, ii, V, I progression in the key indicated. Label all chords with chord names and Roman numerals.

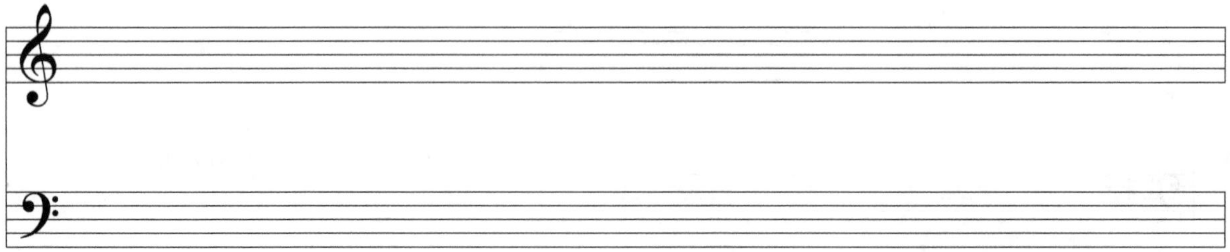

D♭ Major

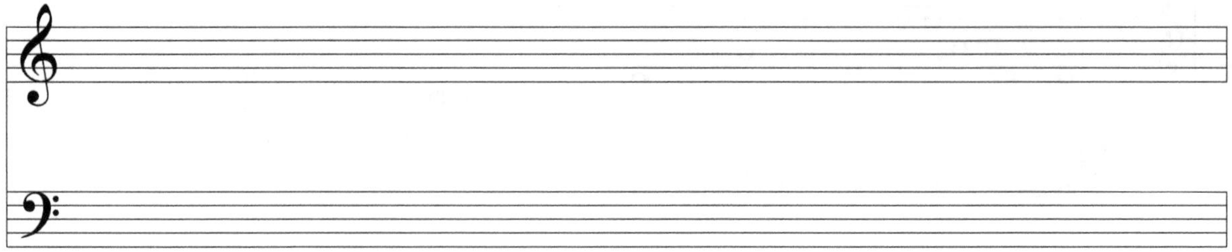

F Major

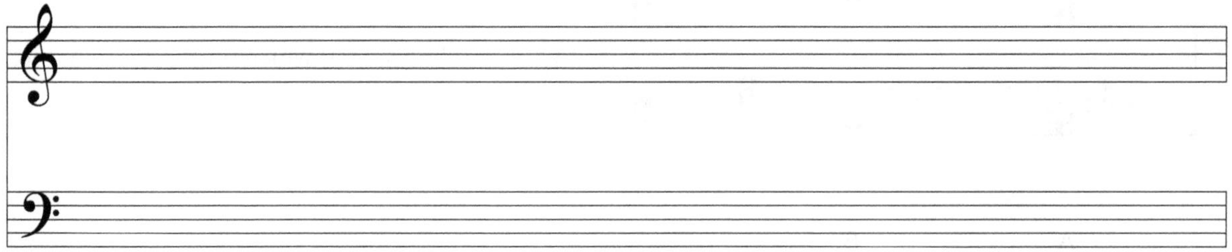

E Major

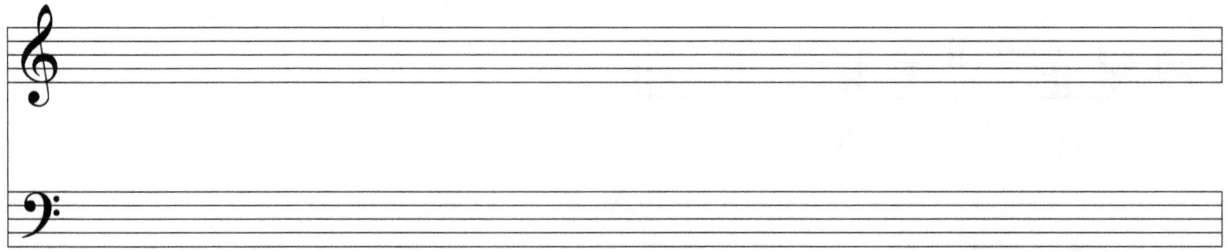

G Major

Inversions

HELPFUL HINTS

1. The notes that make up the chord always stay the same. It is only the order of the notes that changes.
2. When naming chords that are in inversions, the chord name *always* comes first.
3. The first inversion chord has the third on the bottom.
4. The second inversion chord has the fifth on the bottom.

Eb — root position   Eb/G — 1st inversion   Eb/Bb — 2nd inversion

C- — root position   C-/Eb — 1st inversion   C-/G — 2nd inversion

Draw the following chords in root position, first inversion, and second inversion. Label each chord.

F augmented

A diminished

B major

E minor

Choral Analysis

You will often see chords broken up into an SATB configuration for group numbers. The inversion is still based on the lowest note (in most cases that is the bass part).

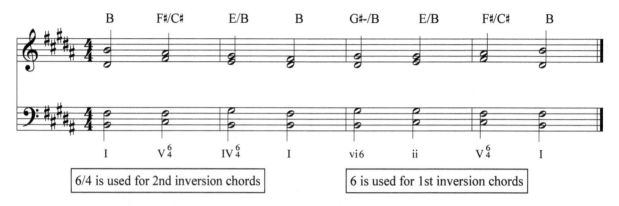

6/4 is used for 2nd inversion chords   6 is used for 1st inversion chords

---

HELPFUL HINTS

1. Re-draw the notes of each chord to build a snowman and then figure out the name of the chord. You can also draw all of the chords in the key on a piece of scrap paper—that way you know what your choices are.
2. Label the chord names first and then the Roman numerals. If you know the name of the chord and the bass note, it will be easier to assign the appropriate Roman numeral.

Label all of the chords with chord names and roman numerals. Sing through with a group if possible.

Performance Tips

The Music Department

Did you know that it takes an entire music team to put up a Broadway show? I am sure you have heard of the composer and the music director, but what about these other jobs?

Composer: The composer writes the music. The composer creates the melody and harmony that all of the other musical work is based on.

Music supervisor: The music supervisor is in charge of the Music department. The music supervisor works with the producer and director to put together the music team for the show and oversees all musical decisions (arrangements, orchestrations, casting, etc.).

Music director: The music director teaches the music to the cast. They make musical decisions for phrasing, blend, breaths, articulation, cut-offs, and diction. Usually, the music director also rehearses the band and conducts performances of the show. In smaller productions, the duties of the music supervisor are also covered by the music director.

Arranger: An arranger takes the composer's work and arranges it to fit the show. This may mean a change in style, the addition of an introduction or ending, or making chord substitutions in the harmonic structure. The arranger also may compose counter melodies and arrange vocal parts to change a piece from a solo into a duet, trio, or group number.

Orchestrator: The orchestrator takes the music from the arranger and decides which instruments are best suited to play each part. They choose the colors and combinations of instruments that will best suit each piece.

Copyist: The copyist writes out the sheet music. They keep the music updated based on any changes that are made in rehearsals by the music supervisor and/or music director. Before the age of computers, they wrote out each part by hand. Now with computer notation software programs, making changes to the score (and all of the orchestra parts) is not as daunting as it once was, but it is still time consuming. Some shows will have a number of copyists working at one time to incorporate the changes as quickly as possible.

Rehearsal pianist: The rehearsal pianist plays the piano (accompanies) during rehearsal. They have the responsibility of acting as an entire orchestra to support the cast during rehearsals.

17

Dominant Seventh Chords; V of V Chords; Suspended Chords; Song Analysis

Seventh Chords

A seventh chord goes beyond the triad by adding a fourth note to the chord. The added note is a third above the top note of the triad (the fifth of the chord). It is also a seventh from the root of the chord (hence the name seventh chord). The first type of seventh chord we will look at is the **dominant seventh chord**.

The dominant seventh chord is built using a major triad as the base and adding a minor third to the top. This creates an outer interval of a minor seventh.

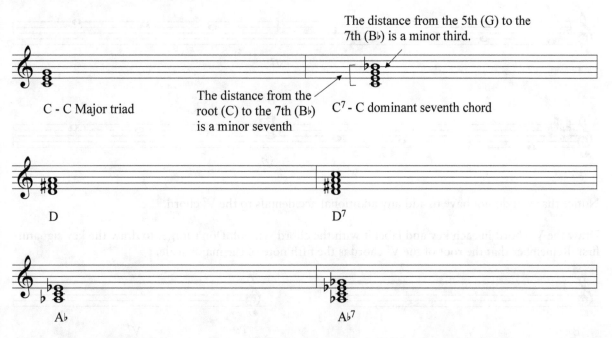

The distance from the 5th (G) to the 7th (B♭) is a minor third.

The distance from the root (C) to the 7th (B♭) is a minor seventh

C - C Major triad

C⁷ - C dominant seventh chord

D

D⁷

A♭

A♭⁷

Seventh chords, like triads, are made up of thirds stacked on one another. It is helpful to draw the four notes on the staff first (the "snowman") and then add the accidentals. Remember the dominant seventh is a major triad with a minor third on top. Starting from the bottom you have a M3, m3, and m3.

Draw the indicated dominant seventh chords.

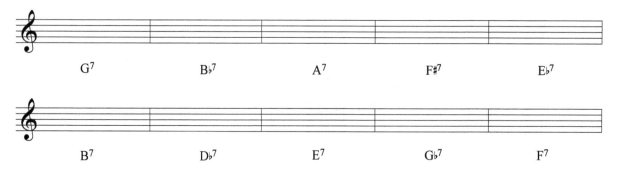

You can find a dominant seventh chord in every major key. It is built on the fifth scale degree.

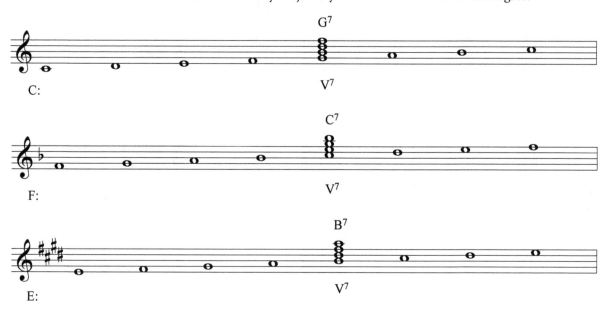

Notice that you do not have to add any additional accidentals to the V⁷ chord.

Draw the V⁷ chord in each key and label it with the chord symbol. Don't forget to draw the key signature first. Remember that the root of the V⁷ chord is the fifth note of the major scale.

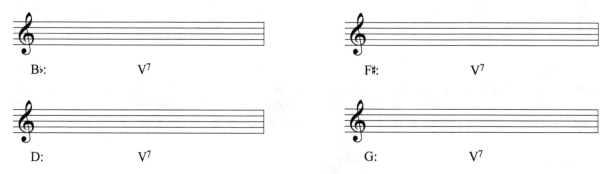

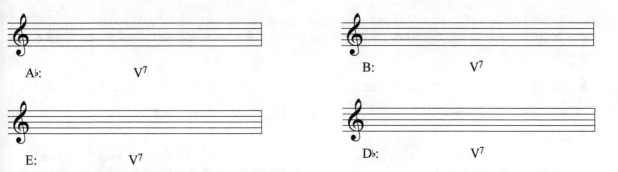

Ab: V⁷   B: V⁷

E: V⁷   Db: V⁷

Seventh chords can be found in root position, first, second, or third inversion.

Take a look at the G⁷ chord which is the V⁷ chord in C major.

G⁷   G⁷/B   G⁷/D   G⁷/F

V 7   V ⁶₅   V ⁴₃   V ⁴₂

The inversions are the same in every key. Here is the E⁷ chord which is the V⁷ in A major.

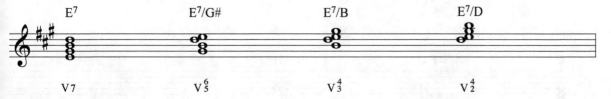

E⁷   E⁷/G#   E⁷/B   E⁷/D

V 7   V ⁶₅   V ⁴₃   V ⁴₂

Draw the following seventh chords in first inversion and label them appropriately.

B⁷   F⁷   Db⁷   E⁷   C#⁷

Draw the following seventh chords in second inversion and label them appropriately.

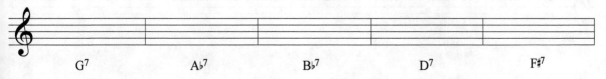

G⁷   Ab⁷   Bb⁷   D⁷   F#⁷

Draw the following seventh chords in third inversion and label them appropriately.

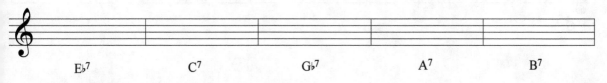

Eb⁷   C⁷   Gb⁷   A⁷   B⁷

The V⁷ chord often replaces the V chord in chord progressions such as the I, IV, V, I and the I, vi, ii, V, I. It has a strong pull to the one chord with the addition of the seventh that moves to the third of the I chord.

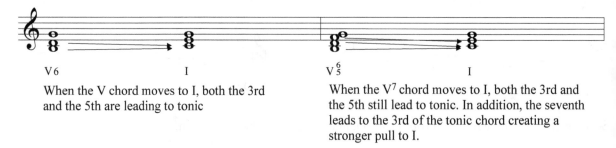

When the V chord moves to I, both the 3rd and the 5th are leading to tonic

When the V⁷ chord moves to I, both the 3rd and the 5th still lead to tonic. In addition, the seventh leads to the 3rd of the tonic chord creating a stronger pull to I.

Listen to the following two progressions. Can you hear the difference between the V chord and the V⁷?

Example 17-1

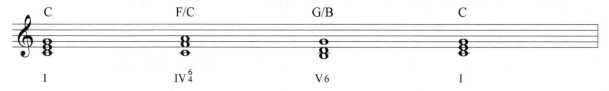

Example 17-2

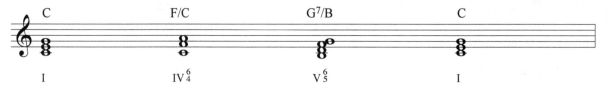

Practice drawing the I, IV, V⁷, I progression in the keys indicated. Use smooth voice leading. Label the chords with both Roman numerals and chord symbols. Don't forget to draw the key signature first!

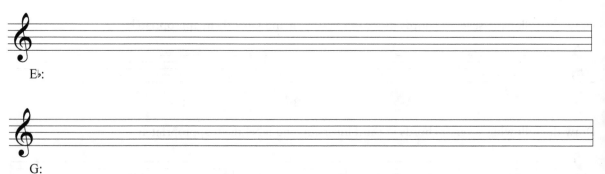

B:

D♭:

A:

Listen to the following two progressions. Can you hear the difference between the V chord and the V⁷?

Example 17-3

Example 17-4

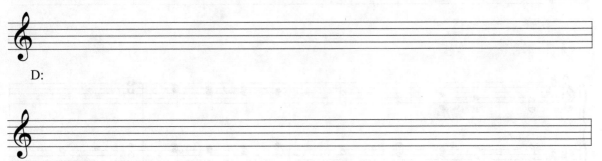

Practice drawing the I, vi, ii, V⁷, I progression in the keys indicated. Use smooth voice leading. Label the chords with both Roman numerals and chord symbols. Don't forget to draw the key signature first!

D:

F:

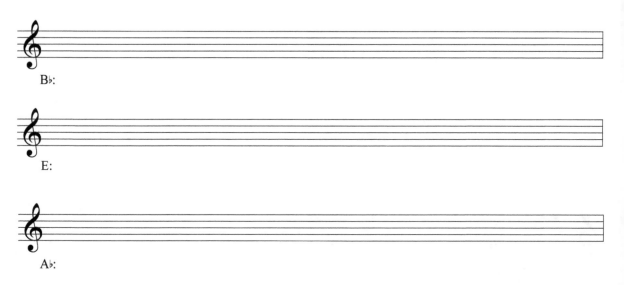

B♭:

E:

A♭:

Analyze each chord with chord names above and Roman numerals below. Sing through each part and then sing with a group if possible. Can you hear the difference between the major and minor chords and inversions?

V of V Chords

As we have learned, the V chord (dominant) serves the function of pulling us to I (tonic). In some cases you will find major triads or dominant seventh chords that are acting as the V (dominant) in a different key from the key you are in. The song is not **modulating** to a new key, but does offer some new colors and is often bringing the song around the circle of fifths (that again)!

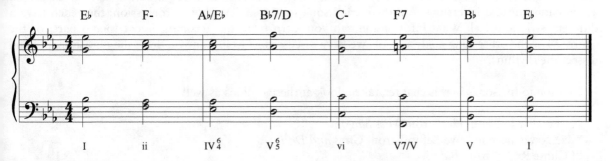

Here the F7 chord is the dominant seventh chord in the key of B♭. Since B♭ is the V chord in the key of E♭, we label it as a V7/ V (the V7 of the V).

You will also find V and V7 chords that relate to other chords in the key. In the example below you will see a V7/ii as well as a V/V.

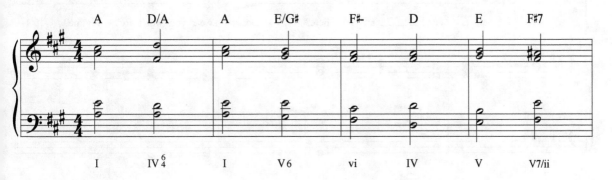

Song Analysis

Analyze the chords and label them with chord names above and Roman numerals below. Listen to a recording and sing through each example. You have seen some of these excerpts before without the proper accompaniment and inversions. Although each song uses a similar chord progression, they each have a different style and feel. What information can you learn from the **accompaniment** (piano part) or the chords? Use the other song analysis tools we have discussed as well. Can you draw the phrase shapes and dissect the rhythms?

In addition to the songs in this chapter, take a look at these options as well.

"Now That I've Seen Her" from *Miss Saigon*.
"I've Never Been in Love Before" from *Guys and Dolls*.
"I Chose Right" from *Baby*.
"Let's Hear it For the Boy" from *Footloose*.

"Summer Nights" from *Grease*

Jim Jacobs
Warren Casey

found you would you   let me come and   stay?

She swam by me,   she got a cramp ..   He ran by me,   got my suit damp.

Saved her life,   she near-ly drowned.   He showed off,   splash-ing a-round.

Sum-mer sun,   some-thing's be-gun___ then,   oh,   oh, those sum-mer nights.

Suspended Chords

Suspended chords are chords that substitute the second or the fourth for the third. Often the suspended chord resolves to a major or minor triad. Suspended chords create tension and allow for resolution.

Observe the suspended chords below. Suspended chords are labeled with a *sus2* or *sus4* depending on the note that is used to create the suspension.

In the Csus4 you have the root (C) and the fifth (G) but instead of the third (E), there is a fouth (F).

In the Csus2 you have the root (C) and the fifth (G) but instead of the third (E), there is a second (D).

Listen to example 17-5 to hear both sus4 and sus2 chords.

Observe the suspended chords below as they resolve to the major triad.

Listen to example 17-6 to hear a sus4 and a sus2 chord resolve to the major triad.

*The fourth in a sus chord is a perfect fourth above the root of the chord. The second is a major second above the root of the chord.

Practice drawing the following sus chords. The first one is done for you.

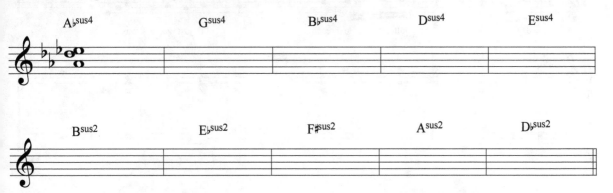

Continue the song analysis from earlier in the chapter. Pay special attention to the suspended chords in this example. How do they add to the mood?

"Leavin's Not The Only Way To Go" from *Big River*   Roger Miller

18

Minor Key Signatures and Natural Minor Scales

Minor Keys

There are fifteen **minor keys** in Western music. Each minor key has a **relative** major key that shares the same key signature. The relationship between a minor key and its relative major is a minor third. The minor key is a minor third *below* the relative major key.

See the circle of fifths below. The minor keys are found inside the circle adjacent to their relative major keys.

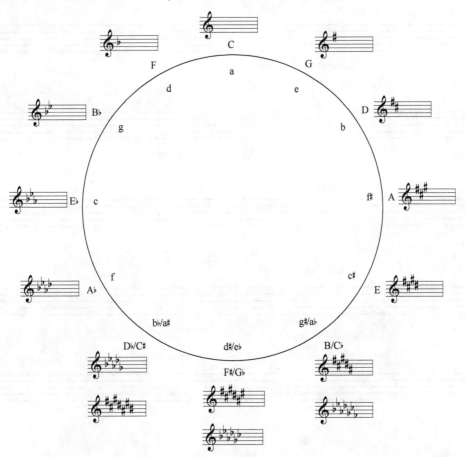

Draw a treble clef and the following minor key signatures.

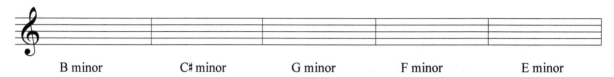

B minor   C♯ minor   G minor   F minor   E minor

Identify the following minor key signatures.

Draw the following **natural minor scales** using a key signature. A natural minor scale uses the notes that are found in the key signature.

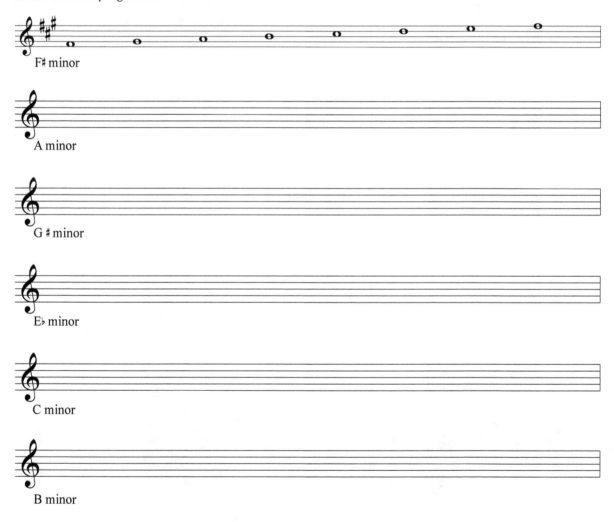

F♯ minor

A minor

G ♯ minor

E♭ minor

C minor

B minor

Minor Scales vs. Major Scales

As we discussed in Chapter 3, the formula for a major scale is WWHWWWH. The formula for a natural minor scale is WHWWHWW.

See the examples below:

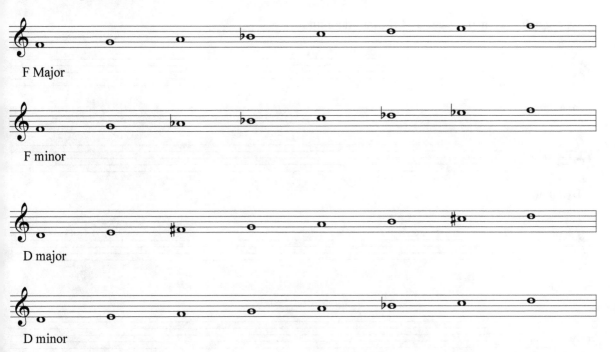

These are called **parallel minor** scales. They use the same set of notes on the staff but the accidentals are different.

To move from a major scale to a minor scale, you need to lower the third, sixth, and seventh scale degrees by a half step. Take a look at the following G major scale and its parallel minor—G minor.

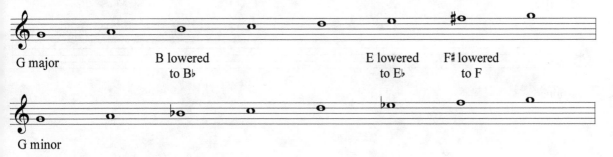

HELPFUL HINTS

When you are lowering a note, you don't always need to add a flat (♭). If you are lowering a sharp note, you need to add a natural instead.

Draw the indicated major scale and the parallel minor.

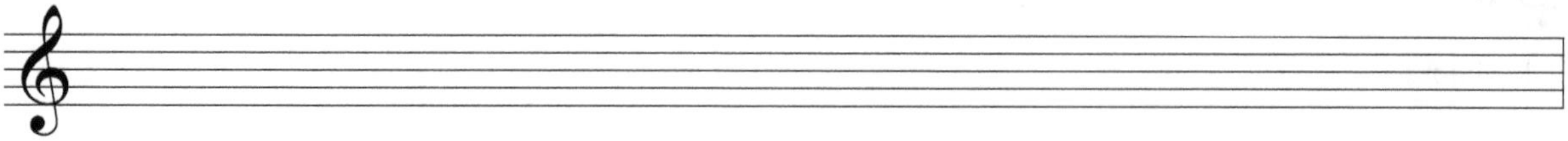

B♭ major

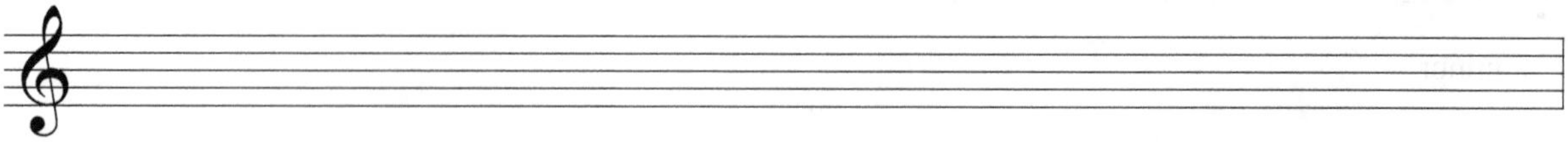

B♭ minor

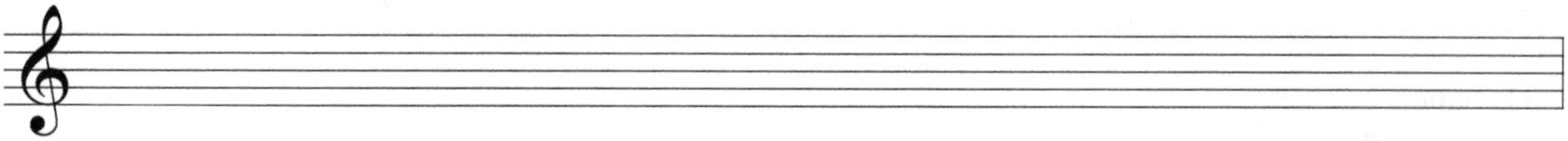

E major

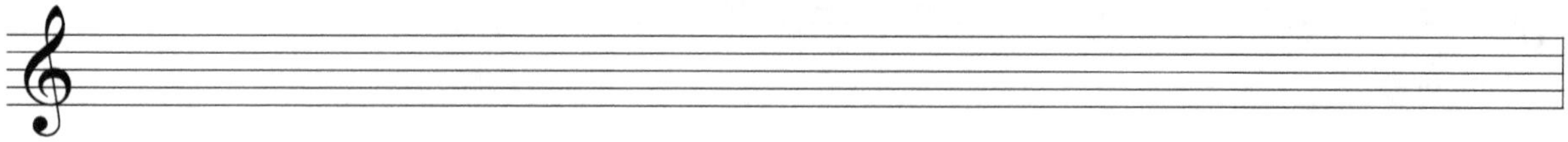

E minor

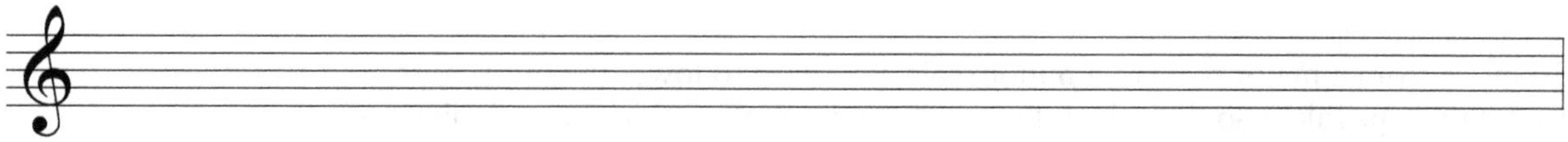

A♭ major

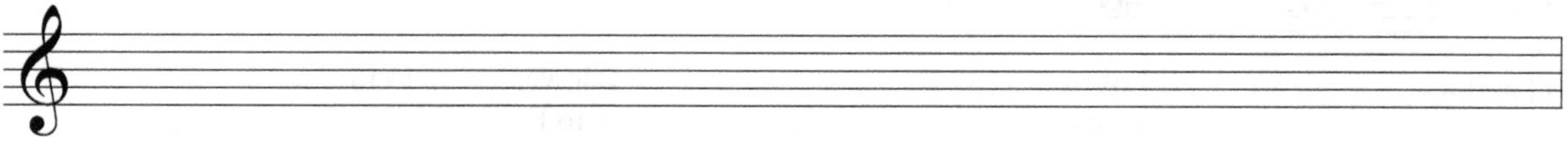

A♭ minor

C♯ Major

C♯ minor

Parallel Minor and Relative Minor

A minor key/scale is the same no matter which way you think about it. The terms relative and parallel focus on the relationship of the minor key/scale to the major key/scale. Let's look at a few examples.

B minor scale

D major is the relative major key because it shares the same key signature as B minor.

B major is the parallel major key because it shares the same tonic (B) and runs parallel to B minor on the staff (although the accidentals are different).

Or you can think about it starting with the major key:

A♭ major scale

F minor is the relative minor because it shares the same key signature.

A♭ minor is the parallel minor because it shares the same tonic (A♭) and runs parallel to A♭ major on the staff (although the accidentals are different).

Relative keys share a key signature (much like relatives share some DNA).

Parallel keys share tonic and run parallel to each other on the staff (like two trains running on the same track but making different stops).

Sight-Singing

The solfege syllables for a minor scale are adjusted because of the lowered third, sixth, and seventh. The new syllables, Me, Le, and Te, should rhyme with may. Practice singing the C minor scale seen below and then try more minor scales. It may take a while to get this new sound in your head. Listen to Example 18-1 to hear a minor scale played on the piano.

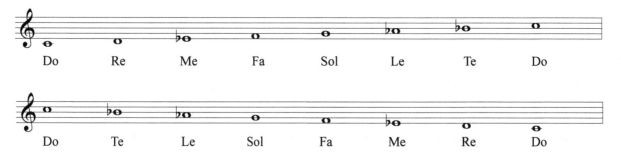

Do   Re   Me   Fa   Sol   Le   Te   Do

Do   Te   Le   Sol   Fa   Me   Re   Do

Sing the following minor melodies using solfege and listen to the first four examples on the website.

Example 18-2

Example 18-3

Example 18-4

Example 18-5

19

Harmonic Minor Scales and Melodic Minor Scales; Song Analysis

Minor Scales

The minor scale that we looked at in Chapter 18 is called the natural minor scale (it occurs naturally in the minor key). When working in a minor key, you will also find a harmonic minor scale. The harmonic minor scale uses a raised seventh scale degree. The raised seventh scale degree changes the harmonic structure to give us a dominant V chord and a diminished vii° chord in the minor key which pull the listener to tonic.

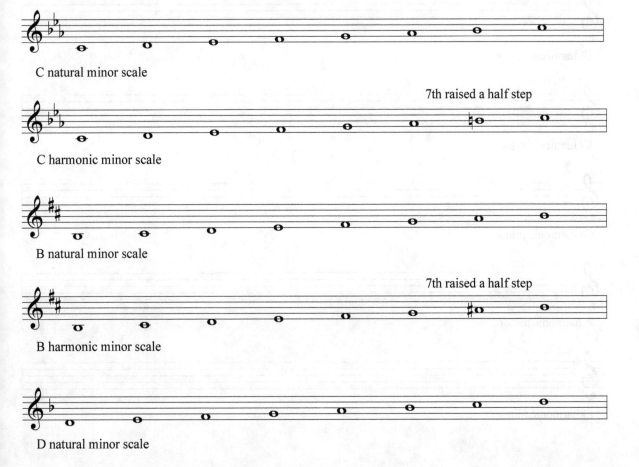

C natural minor scale

7th raised a half step

C harmonic minor scale

B natural minor scale

7th raised a half step

B harmonic minor scale

D natural minor scale

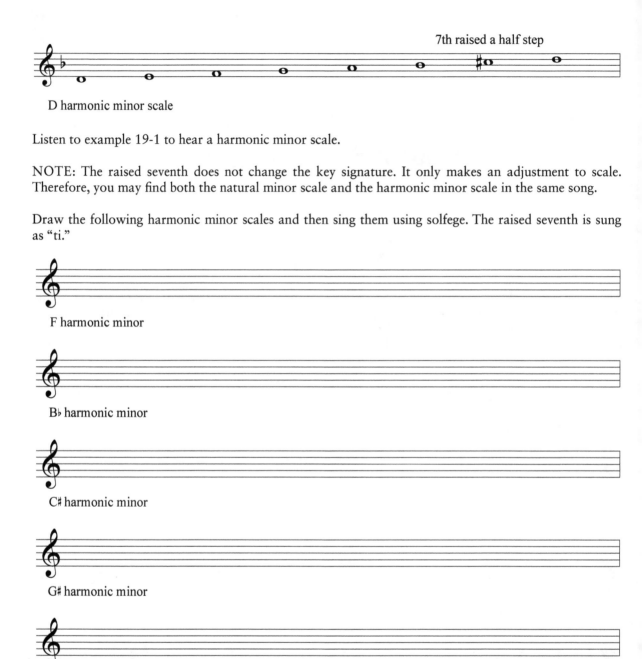

D harmonic minor scale

Listen to example 19-1 to hear a harmonic minor scale.

NOTE: The raised seventh does not change the key signature. It only makes an adjustment to scale. Therefore, you may find both the natural minor scale and the harmonic minor scale in the same song.

Draw the following harmonic minor scales and then sing them using solfege. The raised seventh is sung as "ti."

F harmonic minor

B♭ harmonic minor

C♯ harmonic minor

G♯ harmonic minor

A harmonic minor

E♭ harmonic minor

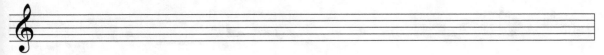

F# harmonic minor

G harmonic minor

Sight-Singing

Sing the following melodies using solfege.

The third type of minor scale is a **melodic minor** scale. In this scale, the sixth and seventh scale degrees are raised a half step when the scale is ascending. They are lowered back to their original pitch when the scale is descending. Listen to example 19-2 to hear a melodic minor scale.

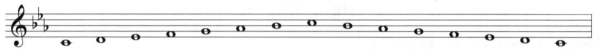

C natural minor scale

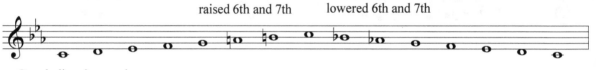

C melodic minor scale

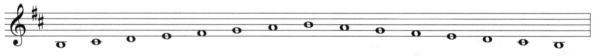

B natural minor scale

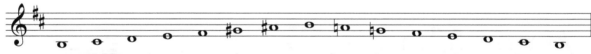

B melodic minor scale

D natural minor scale

D melodic minor scale

When drawing a melodic minor scale, you must always draw it ascending and descending.

Draw the following melodic minor scales and then sing them using solfege. The raised sixth and seventh are sung as "la" and "ti" respectively.

E melodic minor

A♭ melodic minor

G melodic minor

C♯ melodic minor

F melodic minor

B♭ melodic minor

D♯ melodic minor

F♯ melodic minor

Sight-Singing

Sing the following melodies using solfege.

8.

Song Analysis

Listen to a recording of the following songs and then sing through each melody. What minor scale do you hear? Why do you think the song was written in a minor key? Does it stay minor the whole time? Does the key and/or key change support the lyrics and the emotional arc of the song?

"The Devil You Know" from *Sideshow*

Bill Russell
Henry Krieger

We don't work in the best of sit-u-a - tions. We don't live___ ver-y well.___

We don't live___ in the neigh-bor-hood of heav-en. We live some - where / clos-er to hell.

See the raised "ti?" This uses the harmonic scale.

"Pulled" from *The Addams Family*

Andrew Lippa

I don't have a sun-ny dis-po - si-tion. I'm not known for be-ing too a-mused.

My de-mean-or's locked in one po - si-tion. See my face? I'm en-thused.

Sud-den-ly, how-ev-er, I've been puzz-led. Bun-ny rab-bits make me want to cry.

All my in-hi-bi-tions have been muzz-led and I think I know why.

Why is there an f# in the "bunny rabbits" measure? What is changing in Wednesday's world that may be the reason for the added accidentals in the last 5 measures of this excerpt? Continue listening to the song? What key do we move to for the chorus immediately after this excerpt? Why?

"Far From the Home I Love" from *Fiddler On The Roof*

Jerry Bock
Sheldon Harnick

"Far from the Home I Love" also shifts from a minor key into a major key. In this example, we are moving from C minor to C major and the key signature is adjusted for the different phrases. In this excerpt, the minor section is asking difficult questions while the major section is reminiscing about a place that she loves. Listen to the rest of the song. Does she end in major or minor? How does this impact the decision she has to make?

Additional songs to study:

"No One Mourns the Wicked" from *Wicked*. You can hear the switch from minor to major when Glinda comes in with "And Goodness Knows." How does this help shift the mood?

"Pulled" from *The Addams Family*. Listen for the shift from major to minor when she goes into "I'm being pulled in a new . . ." What does this change tell us about Wednesday's point of view at this moment?

"Soliloquy" from *Carousel*. This piece shifts from minor to major as Billy contemplates what it will be like to have a child. What sections are in a minor key? Major key? How does this help the actor and the audience follow his journey? Also, listen to the changes in rhythm and accompaniment for further insight into Billy's emotional arc through the song.

Listening

Listen to each scale played in example 19-3. Determine the type of minor scale that you hear.

1. harmonic minor
2. natural minor
3. melodic minor
4.
5.
6.
7.
8.
9.
10.
11.
12.
13.
14.
15.

Listen to example 19-4 and write the minor melody that you hear.

Listen to example 19-5 and write the minor melody that you hear.

Listen to example 19-6 and write the minor melody that you hear.

Listen to example 19-7 and write the minor melody that you hear.

20

Minor Chord Progressions; Song Analysis

In each minor key you will find three minor triads. These triads are built on the first, fourth, and fifth notes of the natural minor scale. Similar to our work in the major keys, you do not need to add any accidentals to the chords since they already appear in the key signature. See below where the chords are labeled with Roman numerals and chord names.

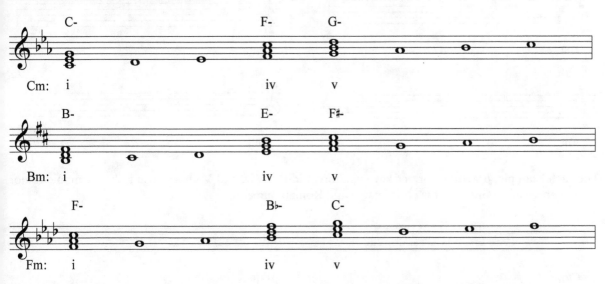

If you use the harmonic minor scale, the minor v chord becomes a major V chord when you raise the seventh scale degree. Since we are not changing the key signature, you must use an accidental to make the adjustment.

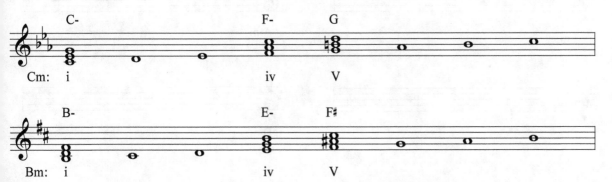

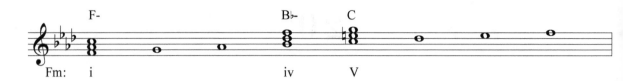

For each example, draw the correct key signature and the i, iv, and v chords using the natural minor scale. Label each chord with the chord name and Roman numeral.

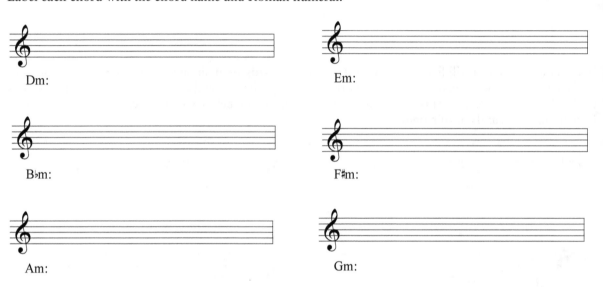

For each example, draw the correct key signature and the i, iv, and V chords using the harmonic minor scale. Label each chord with the chord name and Roman numeral.

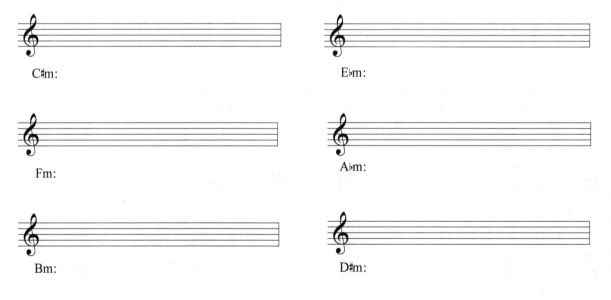

As we found with major keys, you can draw a triad on each scale degree to find chords of different qualities. When using the natural minor scale, the chord qualities are i, ii°, III, iv, v, VI, VII, i.

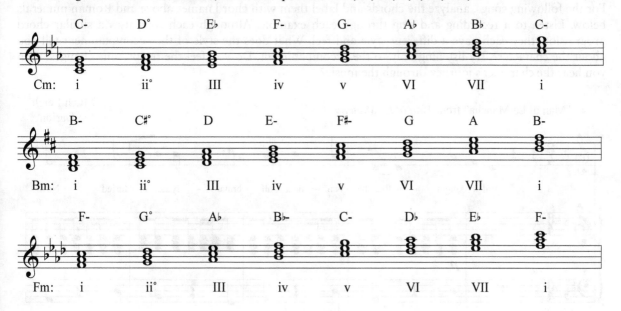

When using the harmonic minor scale, the chord qualities are i, ii°, III+, iv, V, VI, #vii°, i. Remember that songs in minor keys may use more than one type of minor scale.

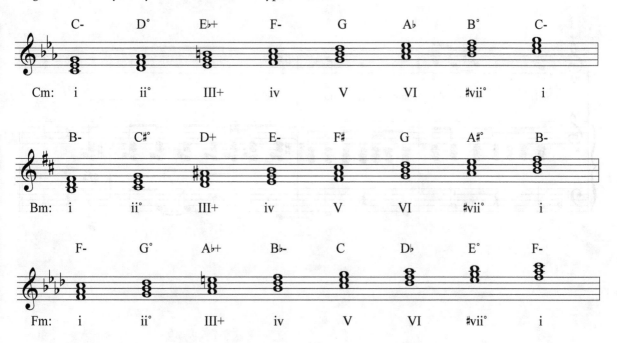

Song Analysis

For the following songs, analyze the chords and label them with chord names above and Roman numerals below. Listen to a recording and sing through each example. Although each song uses a similar chord progression, they each have a different style and feel. What does the style of the accompaniment tell you about the character? Try listening only to the accompaniment. Do you feel the tempo/time changes? Can you hear the character's journey through the music?

"Man of La Mancha" from *Man of La Mancha*

Mitch Leigh
Joe Darion

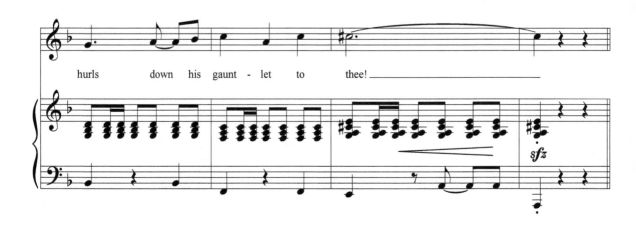

"I Will Prevail" from *Wonderland: A New Alice*   Frank Wildhorn
                                                                    Jack Murphy

When using a melodic minor scale, the chord qualities are i, ii, III+, IV, V, vi°, #vii°, i.

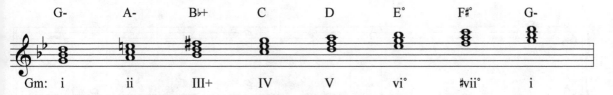

"Your Daddy's Son" from *Ragtime*

Lynn Ahrens
Stephen Flaherty

Write a melody to go with the following chord progressions. Label the chords with chord names above and
Roman numerals below. Sing the melody using solfege while playing the chords.

Review of Chapters 17–20 and Performance Tips (Song Form)

Dominant Seventh Chords

These are built with a major triad on the bottom and a minor third on top of that. Remember to build your snowman first and then work on the intervals.

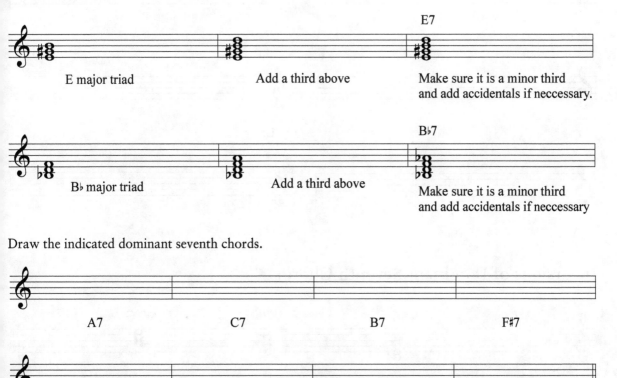

E major triad

Add a third above

E7

Make sure it is a minor third and add accidentals if neccessary.

B♭ major triad

Add a third above

B♭7

Make sure it is a minor third and add accidentals if neccessary

Draw the indicated dominant seventh chords.

A7   C7   B7   F#7

D♭7   G7   E♭7   C#7

You can also build a dominant seventh chord in a major key. The dominant seventh chord is built on the fifth note of the scale.

Remember when you are working in a major key you don't have to add any accidentals to the V7 chord. The key signature takes care of it for you.

Draw the indicated key signature and then a I, IV, V7, I progression in that key. Label the chords with chord names above and Roman numerals below.

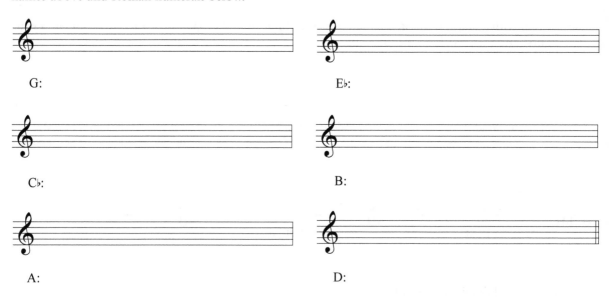

G:

Eb:

Cb:

B:

A:

D:

Inversions of Dominant Seventh Chords

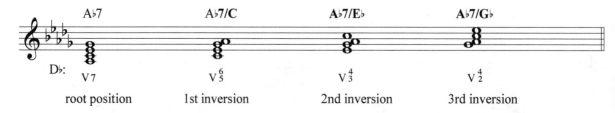

REMEMBER: The notes in the chord stay the same in an inversion—only the order is changed.

Draw the key signature and then the V7 chord in root position, first, second, and third inversions. Label all of the chords with chord names on top and Roman numerals on the bottom.

B♭:

E:

G♭:

F:

C♯:

HELPFUL HINTS

1. The name of the chord comes first (with the 7) before the slash and the bass note to show inversion.
2. You may want to make a snowman out of the notes to help determine the name of the chord.
3. Remember, you are looking at all of the notes in both the treble clef and bass clef.

Choral Analysis with Dominant Seventh Chords

Label all chords with chord names on top and Roman numerals on the bottom.

Minor Key Signatures

Draw a complete circle of fifths with major keys on the outside and minor keys on the inside.

Draw a treble clef and the indicated minor key signature.

G minor   D minor   F♯ minor   C minor

A♭ minor   E minor   B minor   G♯ minor

Minor Scales

HELPFUL HINTS

1. Always start by drawing the minor key signature.
2. Next, draw the eight note scale starting on "do" in that key.
3. If it a natural minor scale, you are finished.
4. If it is a harmonic minor scale, raise the seventh. That may mean adding a sharp or a natural depending on the original note.
5. If it is a melodic minor scale, don't forget to draw the scale descending as well as ascending.
You need to raise the sixth and the seventh on the way up and lower them back to their original pitches on the way down.

Draw the indicated minor scale.

A harmonic minor

B♭ melodic minor

E natural minor

G melodic minor

F natural minor

C# harmonic minor

Choral Analysis in a Minor Key

Analyze the chords in the exercises below. Use both chord names and Roman numerals. Sing each example with a group if possible.

Performance Tips

Song Form

Most songs are divided into sections musically and lyrically. Usually you will find a verse and a chorus. In general, the lyrics for the verse change each time the verse appears while the lyrics for the chorus tend to stay the same or similar. Some songs may also have a bridge and/or a coda section. A verse or chorus is usually eight to sixteen bars long.

Take a listen/look at "Sit Down You're Rockin' the Boat" from the original *Guys and Dolls*. It starts with an eight-bar verse ("I dreamed last night . . .") and then goes into the chorus at "For the people all said . . ." This is a nineteen-bar chorus (sixteen bars of vocals and three bars of transition). After the transition, we are back to another verse with new lyrics and then a second chorus. The second chorus is sixteen bars long (no transition) and has slightly modified lyrics ("people all said beware . . ."). Next, you hear a third verse with new lyrics and then a final chorus where the lyrics are in the first person ("I said to myself . . ."). At the end of the third chorus, we go into a six-bar bridge section. This section has repetitive lyrics and a slightly different feel than anything we have heard so far, with syncopation in the vocals and a pedal tone (held note) in the orchestra. After the bridge, we end with an eight-bar coda. The coda is an extension of the lyrics and musical ideas of the chorus but it builds to a climactic ending.

Notice that each verse is in 4/4 time. The chorus, bridge, and coda are in cut-time.

Overall song form:
Verse 1, Chorus, Verse 2, Chorus, Verse 3, Chorus, Bridge, Coda

Now take a look and listen to "Home" from *Beauty and The Beast*. Here we start with a sixteen-bar verse which feels like an introduction to the song. The chorus begins with "It this home?" and lasts for twenty bars. Next we move into a bridge beginning at "What I'd give" (notice we begin this section on an a minor chord, the vi chord in C, and it briefly feels like we have moved into the relative minor). At the end of the nine-bar bridge we modulate to D major for the second chorus. At the end of the twenty-bar chorus we have a short six-bar coda starting with "My heart's far . . ."

Overall song form:
Verse, Chorus, Bridge, Chorus, Coda

Look at songs that you are working on. What is the song form? Is there more than one verse? How are they different? Does the chorus change each time or stay the same? Is there a bridge or coda? Why have the writers broken up the song in this way? How can this help you understand your character's journey? Does your song have a key change? How does it affect the mood of your song?

21

Major, Minor, Half-Diminished, and Diminished Seventh Chords

In addition to dominant seventh chords, you will also find **major, minor, diminished, and half-diminished seventh chords.** Each seventh chord is built by stacking major and/or minor thirds in a specific pattern.

Major Seventh Chords

A major seventh chord is built using a major triad as the base and adding a major third on the top. This creates an outer interval of a major seventh.
*REMINDER: A major triad is made up of a major third on the bottom and a minor third on the top.

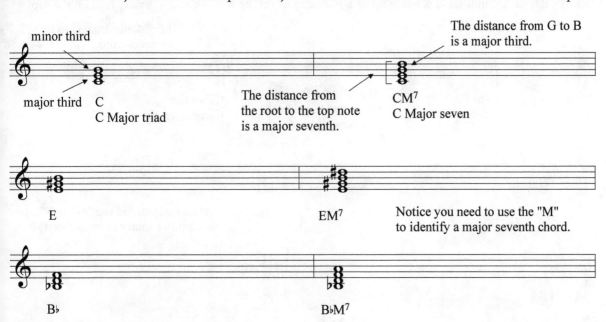

Listen to example 21-1 and you will hear Major 7th chords.

Seventh chords are made up of thirds stacked on top of one another. It is helpful to draw the four notes on the staff first (the "snowman") and then add the accidentals. The pattern for the Major seventh chord is M3, m3, M3 (bottom to top).

Draw the indicated major seventh chords.

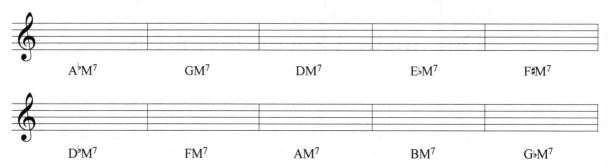

A♭M⁷   GM⁷   DM⁷   E♭M⁷   F♯M⁷

D♭M⁷   FM⁷   AM⁷   BM⁷   G♭M⁷

Minor Seventh Chords

A minor seventh chord is built using a minor triad as the base and adding a minor third on the top. This creates an outer interval of a minor seventh.
*REMINDER: A minor triad is made up of a minor third on the bottom and a major third on the top.

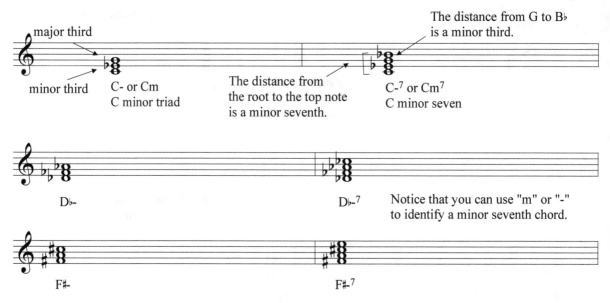

Listen to example 21-2 and you will hear Minor 7th chords.

The pattern for the minor seventh chord is m3, M3, m3 (bottom to top).

Draw the indicated minor seventh chords.

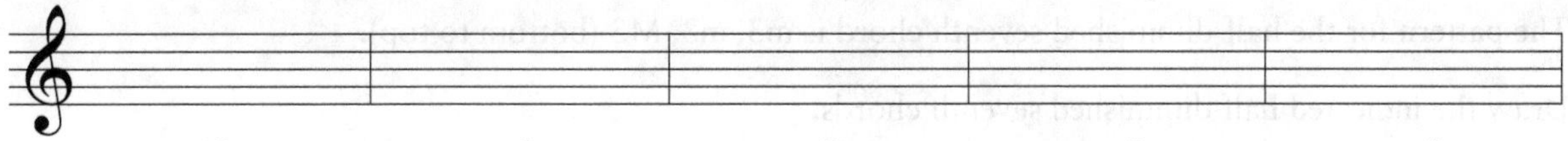

A-^{7} B♭^{7} F-^{7} E-^{7} D-^{7}

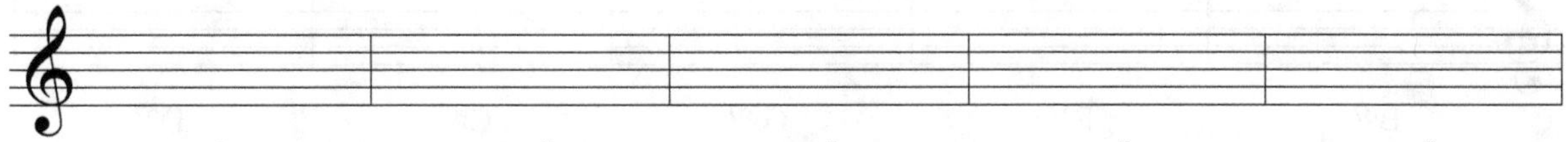

G-^{7} A♭-^{7} B-^{7} G♭-^{7} E♭-^{7}

Identify the following major and minor seventh chords.

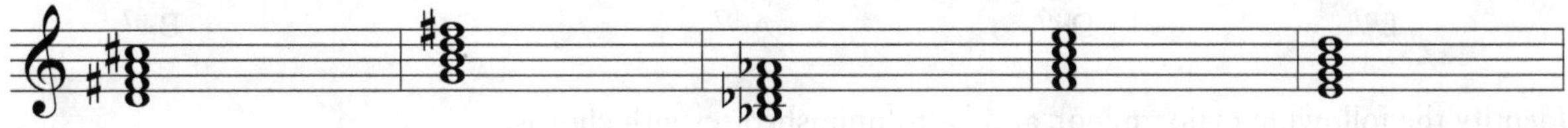

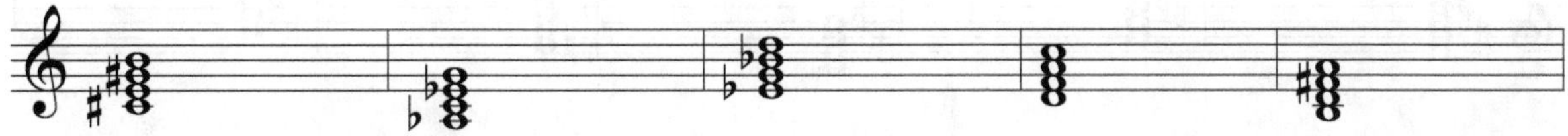

Half-Diminished Seventh Chords

A half-diminished seventh chord is built using a diminished triad as the base and adding a major third on the top. This creates an outer interval of a minor seventh.
*REMINDER: A diminished triad is made up of a minor third on the bottom and a minor third on the top.

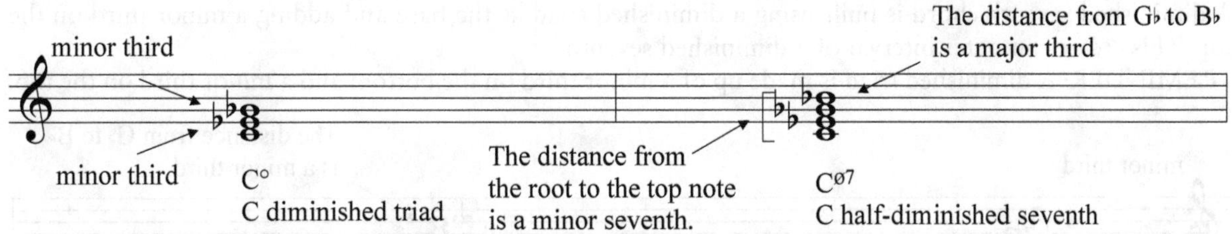
minor third
minor third
The distance from G♭ to B♭
is a major third
The distance from
the root to the top note
is a minor seventh.

C° C diminished triad

C^{ø7} C half-diminished seventh

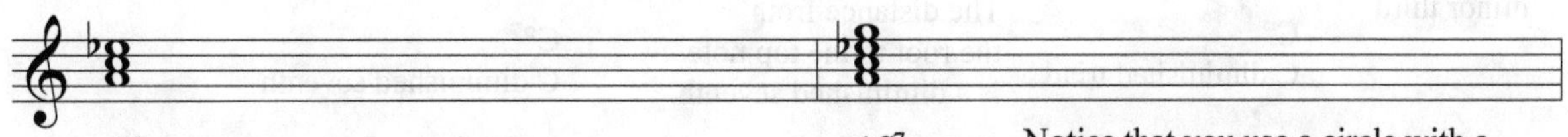

A° A^{ø7}

Notice that you use a circle with a slash through it to identify a half-diminshed seventh chord.

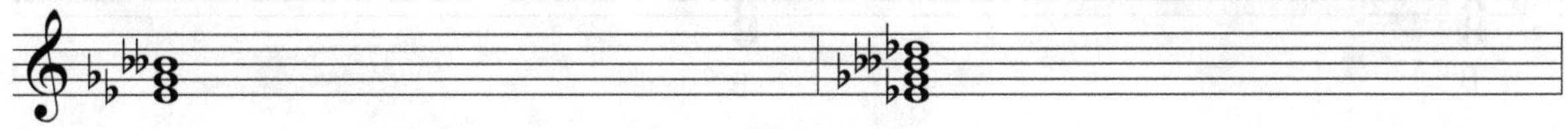

E♭° E♭^{ø7}

Listen to example 21-3 and you will hear half-diminished seventh chords.

The pattern for the half-diminished seventh chord is m3, m3, M3 (bottom to top).

Draw the indicated half-diminished seventh chords.

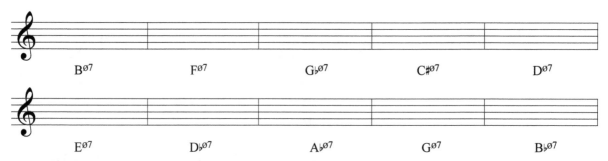

Identify the following major, minor, and half-diminished seventh chords.

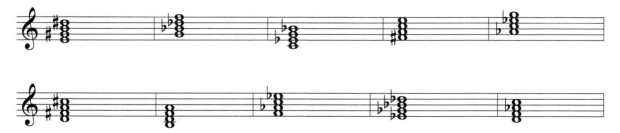

Diminished Seventh Chords

A diminished seventh chord is built using a diminished triad as the base and adding a minor third on the top. This creates an outer interval of a diminished seventh.

*REMINDER: A diminished triad is made up of a minor third on the bottom and a minor third on the top.

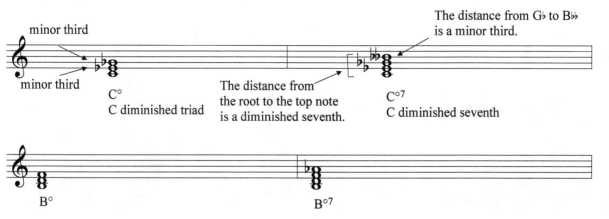

E°   E°7

Listen to example 21-4 and you will hear diminished seventh chords.

The pattern for the diminished seventh chord is m3, m3, m3 (bottom to top).

Draw the indicated diminished seventh chords.

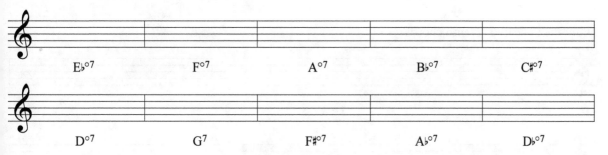

E♭°7   F°7   A°7   B♭°7   C♯°7

D°7   G7   F♯°7   A♭°7   D♭°7

Identify the following major, minor, half-diminished, and diminished seventh chords.

Use the following chart to review all five types of seventh chords.

Chord Type	Chord Symbol	triad quality	seventh quality	quality of thirds
Major 7th	M^7	Major	Major	M3, m3, M3
Dominant 7th	^{7}	Major	Minor	M3, m3, m3
Minor 7th	m^7 or -^{7}	Minor	Minor	m3, M3, m3
Half-Diminished 7th	ø^7	diminished	Minor	m3, m3, M3
Diminished 7th	°^{7}	diminished	diminished	m3, m3, m3

Draw the indicated seventh chords.

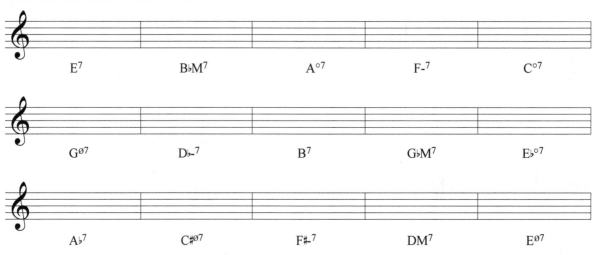

E^7 B♭M^7 A$^{°7}$ F-^{7} C$^{°7}$

G^{ø7} D♭-^{7} B^7 G♭M^7 E♭$^{°7}$

A♭^{7} C♯^{ø7} F♯-^{7} DM^7 E^{ø7}

Identify the following seventh chords.

Analyze the chords in "I Got Rhythm." Examine the use of different types of seventh chords.

"I Got Rhythm" from *Crazy For You*   George and Ira Gershwin

Listening

Listen to example 21-5 and identify each seventh chord.

A. M7	1.	6.	11.	16.	21.
B. Dominant 7	2.	7.	12.	17.	22.
C. m7	3.	8.	13.	18.	23.
D. ø7	4.	9.	14.	19.	24.
E. °7	5.	10.	15.	20.	25.

Listen to example 21-6 and write out the rhythm that you hear.

Listen to example 21-7 and write out the rhythm that you hear.

Listen to example 21-8 and write out the melody that you hear.

Listen to example 21-9 and write out the melody that you hear.

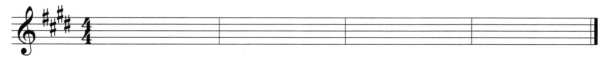

Study the following songs and identify the different types of seventh chords.

"Opening (part 1)" from *Into The Woods*.
"I'm Not at All in Love" from *The Pajama Game*.
"Here I Am" from *Dirty Rotten Scoundrels*.

22

Compound Time

Up to this point we have worked in 4/4, 3/4, and 2/4 time. The quarter note equals one beat in all of these time signatures. We have also worked in cut-time where the half note equals one beat. In this chapter, we will be looking at 6/8, 3/8, 9/8, and 12/8 time. In these time signatures, the eighth note equals one beat.

$\bullet$. = dotted half note = 6 beats

$\bullet$. = dotted quarter note = 3 beats

$\bullet$ = quarter note = 2 beats

$\bullet$ = eighth note = 1 beat

$\bullet$ = sixteenth note = 1/2 beat

These time signatures are called compound time signatures. Compound time signatures are organized in groups of three while simple time signatures (2/4, 3/4, and 4/4) are organized in groups of two. So, although the eighth note equals one beat, music in compound time is often felt in groupings of three eighth notes (or one dotted quarter note).

Therefore, in 6/8 time we have six eighth notes broken up into two groups of three eighth notes each. The accents fall on the first and fourth eighth notes. Many pieces in 6/8 time feel like they are in two with each beat subdivided in groups of three.

Count and clap the following rhythm.

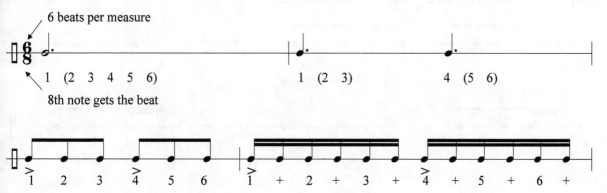

See the accents reinforcing the start of each grouping.

Clap and count the following rhythms. Listen to the examples on the website.

Example 22-1

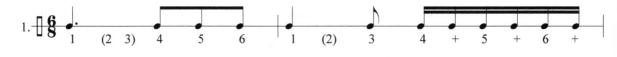

Example 22-2

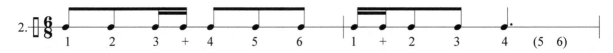

Write in the counts and then count and clap the rhythms.

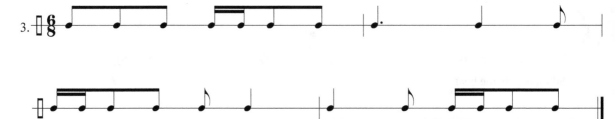

4.

Draw in the bar lines and then clap and count the rhythms.

Fill each measure with the notes indicated. Make sure each measure has six beats.

eighth notes   quarter notes and   dotted quarter notes   dotted half note(s)
                      eighth notes

eighth notes and   quarter notes and   eighth notes and   any combination
sixteenth notes   eighth notes   sixteenth notes

Clap and count the rhythms. Remember that the heavy beats fall on one and four.

1.

2.

3.

Let's look at a few other time signatures where the eighth note equals one beat.

 Three beats in a measure.
The eighth note equals one beat.

Also felt as one big beat, divided in three.

Count and clap the following rhythms.

Nine beats in a measure.
The eighth note equals one beat.

Also felt as three big beats,
divided in three.

Count and clap the following rhythms.

1.
1 (23456) 7 (89)   1   2   3   4 (56) 7 (89)   1 (2) 3   4 (5) 6 7   8   9   1   2 + 3   4 (56)   7 (89)

2.
1 + 2 3   4 (5) 6 7   8 (9) 1 (23) 4   5   6   7 (8) 9   1 (2) 3 4 (5) 6 7 + 8 9   1   2   3   4 (56) 7 (89)

Twelve beats in a measure.
The eighth note equals
one beat.

Also felt as four big beats,
divided in three.

Count and clap the following rhythms.

Sight-Singing

Sing the following melodies using solfege. Look carefully before you start. Some exercises are in minor keys and some are in major keys.

Listening

Listen to example 22-3 and write the rhythm you hear.

Listen to example 22-4 and write the rhythm you hear.

Listen to example 22-5 and write the rhythm you hear.

Listen to example 22-6 and write the melody you hear.

Listen to example 22-7 and write the melody you hear.

Listen to example 22-8 and write the melody you hear.

23

More Compound Time; Song Analysis

In compound time, you will find dotted rhythms and syncopation similar to what we see in simple time. These rhythms help set lyrics closer to the spoken word and they also give music a distinctive feel. All of these choices made by the composer inform the story and character development.

    Look at the following syncopated rhythms. Compare the tied rhythm to the untied rhythm. They sound the same. Clap and count each rhythm and then listen to them on the website.

Example 23-1

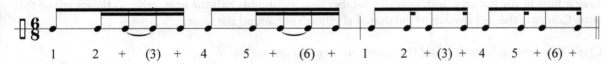

Example 23-2

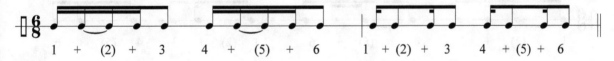

Example 23-3

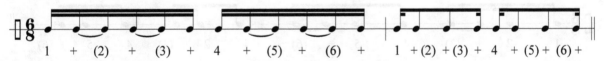

Clap and count each rhythm. Use a metronome to help keep a steady beat.

Take a look at the dotted eighth note. Remember that a dot adds half the note value to the length of that note. Compare the tied rhythm to the dotted rhythm. They sound the same.

Clap and count each rhythm and then listen to them on the website.

Example 23-4

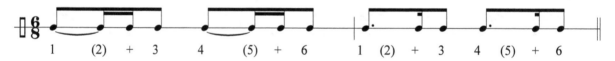

Example 23-5

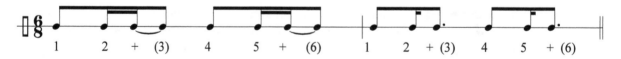

Example 23-6

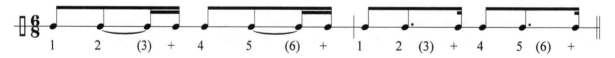

Example 23-7

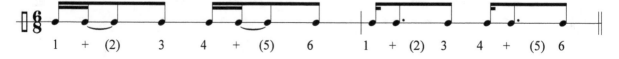

Example 23-8

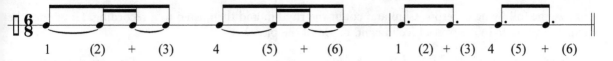

Clap and count the rhythms. Use a metronome to help keep a steady beat.

Song Analysis

Analyze the following excerpts. Clap and count the rhythm and then listen to a recording. How does the rhythm contribute to the overall feeling and mood of the piece?

Sight-Singing

Sing the following melodies using solfege. Use a metronome to keep a steady beat.

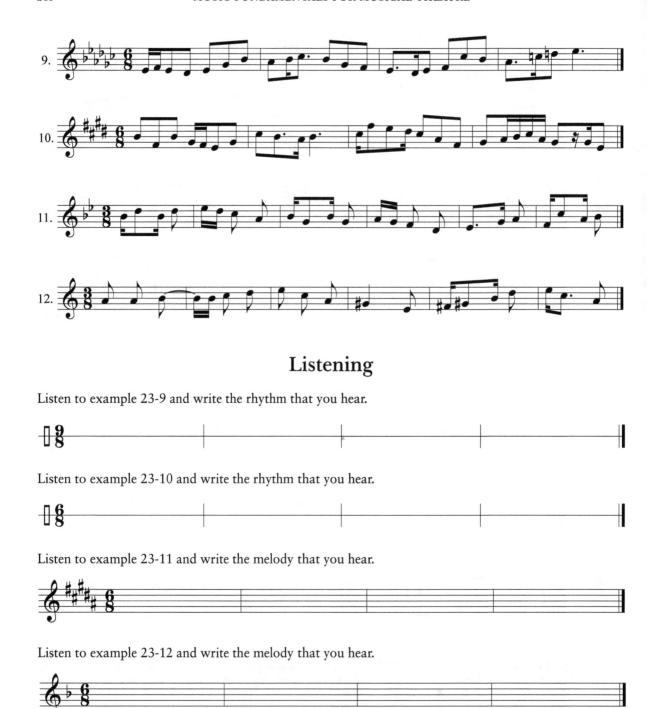

Listening

Listen to example 23-9 and write the rhythm that you hear.

Listen to example 23-10 and write the rhythm that you hear.

Listen to example 23-11 and write the melody that you hear.

Listen to example 23-12 and write the melody that you hear.

24

Song Analysis; Orchestration

Analyzing a Song

We have discussed melody, rhythm, and harmonic structure. We have analyzed songs based on these elements. But what else can the music tell us? What about the accompaniment? What about the orchestra?

When you are working on a song from the musical theatre repertoire, you are often accompanied by a pianist (accompanist). The accompanist is typically playing a piano reduction of the orchestral score. What can you learn from the piano accompaniment? If you are working on a show, you eventually get to the exciting point when the orchestra joins the rehearsal process. Usually that is at the **sitzprobe,** a music rehearsal specifically focused on bringing the actors and orchestra together for the first time. How does that enhance the show or your performance? All of these elements should be taken into consideration when you are working on music.

It is important to listen closely to your musical accompaniment. When listening to the piano alone, listen for things like heavy or driving chords, slow arpeggios, low bass notes and/or high and fast sixteenth notes. What do each of these elements contribute to the musical feel of the piece? When listening to the orchestra, you have the added elements of the different instruments. What instruments are playing? What mood are they setting? Is it romantic or goofy; triumphant or troubled? Does the orchestra give you any clues as to where you are (i.e. Cuba or Texas)?

A Quick Look at the Orchestra

In musical theatre, the size of the orchestra and the choice of instruments can vary drastically from show to show. For the most part, modern pit orchestras are smaller than the traditional pit orchestras of the 1930s–1950s. When traditional shows have a Broadway revival, they are often reorchestrated with a smaller orchestra. This is partially for budgetary purposes but it is largely due to technology. You will find that modern pit orchestras tend to have two or three keyboard synthesizers. The keyboards can be programed to play hundreds of sounds, therefore replacing some "live" instruments. The technology has advanced to a point that some keyboard sounds are sampled from live instruments, creating an authentic sound to most audience members. However, not all shows follow this trend. Currently, *The Phantom of The Opera* is the largest Broadway orchestra, with twenty-seven musicians. *Wicked* and *The Lion King* currently have twenty-three and the revival of *Hello, Dolly!* has twenty-two. All of these shows also have a conductor that doesn't have to play a keyboard part. The rest of the current Broadway orchestras range from six to eighteen musicians (many with a conductor also playing one of the keyboard parts). *Waitress* has the smallest orchestra with six musicians including the pianist /conductor. In no way does the size of an orchestra make a show better or worse. Each show is orchestrated to best serve the music and the storytelling.

What Instruments Are Used?

Traditional orchestras are broken down into four categories:

Strings	Woodwinds	Brass	Percussion
Violin	Piccolo	Trumpet	Bass drum
Viola	Flute	Trombone	Snare drum
Cello	Clarinet	French horn	Timpani
Bass	Oboe		Mallets
Harp	English horn		Cymbals
	Bass clarinet		Drum set
	Bassoon		Auxiliary
	Saxophone		percussion*

*Sometimes a percussionist will have a list of over thirty auxiliary instruments: everything from finger cymbals or wood blocks to a ratchet or mouth siren. Often, these instruments set the sound and the setting for the show. Listen to excerpts from *The Lion King*. There are five percussionists in the orchestra that create the world of the African Pride Lands for the listener. *On Your Feet* has three percussionists to contribute to the Latin feel to the show.

You will also find piano, keyboard(s), and/or guitar(s) in the orchestra. Many modern pit orchestras have a **rhythm section** as the core of the orchestration. The rhythm section typically consists of piano and/or keyboards and/or guitars, bass, and drums.

Babes in Toyland (1903) and *Carousel* (1945)

Let's take a look at two songs from two classic shows. Before we listen to each song, take the time to analyze the sheet music. Follow the steps to become familiar with the material and then answer the questions about the written music.

Steps:
1. Analyze the chords using both chord names and Roman numerals.
2. Clap and count the rhythm of the melody.
3. Read the lyrics.
4. Sing through the melody.
5. Sing the choral parts with a group if possible.
6. Play the piano accompaniment if possible.

Questions:
1. Are there any accidentals or surprising chords (augmented chords in "Graduation Scene")? On what lyric? Does that influence how you sing the phrase?
2. What is the shape of the melodic line? Is it building to a climax?
3. What are the predominant rhythmic patterns in the accompaniment? How do they make you feel? For example, in "Go To Sleep, Slumber Deep" there is syncopation in the left hand – Does it energize you or relax you? In "Graduation Scene" you will find arpeggios throughout the accompaniment. Do they feel jagged or flowing?

"Go To Sleep, Slumber Deep" from *Babes in Toyland*

Victor Herbert
Glen Mac Donough

"Graduation Scene" from *Carousel*

Richard Rodgers
Oscar Hammerstein

Once you have analyzed the written music, listen to a recording with the full orchestra. Write down some of the instruments that you hear on your sheet music and then answer the following questions:

1. What instrument(s) are driving the music? What are the most prominent?
2. What instrument (if any) is doubling the vocal line?
3. Is there a noticeable entrance of a particular instrument or section (e.g. the brass in "Graduation Scene")? How might that influence your performance?
4. Is there an instrument that sticks out that really helps to set the mood or setting of the song (e.g. the celeste in "Go To Sleep, Slumber Deep")?
5. How do the different instruments or families of instruments make you feel? What do they tell you about the setting? What do they tell you about the emotional state of the character(s)?

Kiss Me, Kate (1948 and 1999)

Let's take a look at two versions of one song from the classic show *Kiss Me, Kate*.

The orchestra for the original Broadway production in 1948 and the orchestra for Broadway revival in 1999 were extremely similar in size and instrumentation. Despite those similarities, the new arrangements and orchestrations for the revival provide some major changes to the music. Before we listen to each version of the song "Too Darn Hot," take the time to analyze the sheet music. Follow the same steps as before to become familiar with the material and then answer the questions about the written music.

Steps:
1. Analyze the chords using both chord names and Roman numerals.
2. Clap and count the rhythm of the melody.
3. Read the lyrics.
4. Sing through the melody.
5. Sing the choral parts with a group if possible.
6. Play the piano accompaniment if possible.

Questions:
1. Are there any accidentals, surprising chords, or accented chords for punctuation? On what lyric? Does that influence how you sing the phrase?
2. What is the shape of the melodic line? Is it building to a climax?
3. What are the predominant rhythmic patterns in the accompaniment? How do they make you feel?

"Too Darn Hot" from *Kiss Me, Kate* (1948)   Cole Porter

"Too Darn Hot" from *Kiss Me, Kate* (1999)   Cole Porter

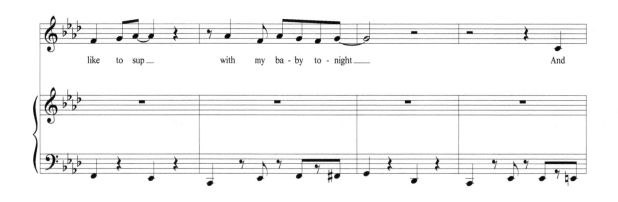

like to sup___ with my ba-by to-night___ And

play the pup___ with my ba-by to-night___ Id

like to sup___ with my ba-by to-night,___ And

Once you have analyzed the written music, listen to a recording of each version with the full orchestra. Write down some of the instruments that you hear on your sheet music and then answer the following questions:

1. What instrument(s) are driving the music? What are the most prominent?
2. What instrument (if any) is doubling the vocal line?
3. Is there a noticeable entrance of a particular instrument or section? How might that influence your performance?
4. Is there an instrument that sticks out that really helps to set the mood or setting of the song?
5. How do the different instruments or families of instruments make you feel? What do they tell you about the setting? What do they tell you about the emotional state of the character(s)?

Children of Eden (1997, Papermill Playhouse, NJ, USA) and *First Date* (2013)

Let's take a look at two relatively contemporary shows with modern orchestra set-ups. *Children of Eden* has twelve musicians while *First Date* has six. They both have three keyboard books and a rhythm section with guitars, keyboards, bass, and drum set. Before we listen to each recording, take the time to analyze the sheet music. Follow the same steps as before to become familiar with the material and then answer the questions about the written music.

Steps:
1. Analyze the chords using both chord names and Roman numerals.
2. Clap and count the rhythm of the melody.
3. Read the lyrics.
4. Sing through the melody.
5. Sing the choral parts with a group if possible.
6. Play the piano accompaniment if possible.

Questions:
1. Are there any accidentals, surprising chords, or accented chords for punctuation? On what lyric? Does that influence how you sing the phrase?
2. What is the shape of the melodic line? Is it building to a climax?
3. What are the predominant rhythmic patterns in the accompaniment? How do they make you feel?

"In the Beginning" from *Children of Eden*   Stephen Schwartz

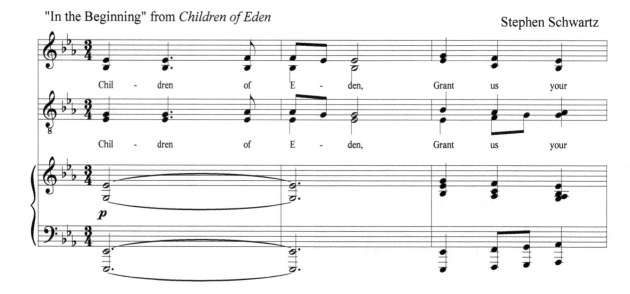

"Safer" from *First Date*

Alan Zachary
Michael Weiner

Once you have analyzed the written music, listen to a recording of each song with the full orchestra. Write down some of the instruments that you hear on your sheet music and then answer the following questions:

1. What instrument(s) are driving the music? What are the most prominent?
2. What instrument (if any) is doubling the vocal line?
3. Is there a noticeable entrance of a particular instrument or section? How might that influence your performance?
4. Is there an instrument that sticks out that really helps to set the mood or setting of the song?
5. How do the different instruments or families of instruments make you feel? What do they tell you about the setting? What do they tell you about the emotional state of the character(s)?

Resources

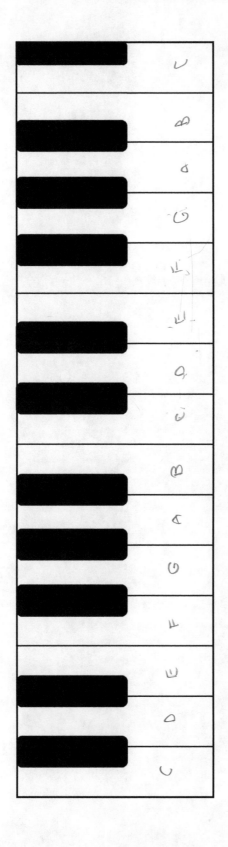

PERMISSIONS ACKNOWLEDGMENTS

The author and publisher gratefully acknowledge the permission granted to reproduce the copyright material in this book:

"Maria" from *West Side Story*
Leonard Bernstein & Steven Sondheim
© Copyright 1956. 1957, 1958. 1959 by Amberson Holdings LLC and Stephen Sondheim. Copyright renewed. Leonard Bernstein Music Publishing Company LLC, publisher. Boosey & Hawkes. Agent for rental.
International copyright secured.

"Somewhere" from *West Side Story*
Leonard Bernstein & Steven Sondheim
© Copyright 1956, 1957, 1958. 1959 by Amberson Holdings LLC and Stephen Sondheim. Copyright renewed. Leonard Bernstein Music Publishing Company LLC, publisher. Boosey & Hawkes, agent for rental.
International copyright secured.

"Almost There" from *The Princess and the Frog*
Music and Lyrics by Randy Newman
© Copyright 2009 Walt Disney Music Company
All Rights Reserved.
Used by Permission.
Reprinted by Permission of Hal Leonard LLC

"Close Every Door" from *Joseph and the Amazing Technicolor® Dreamco*at
Music by Andrew Lloyd Webber
Lyrics by Tim Rice
© Copyright 1969 The Really Useful Group Ltd.
Copyright Renewed
This arrangement © Copyright 2018 The Really Useful Group Ltd.
International Copyright Secured.
All Rights Reserved.
Reprinted by Permission of Hal Leonard LLC

"Come With Me" from *The Boys from Syracuse*
Words by Lorenz Hart
Music by Richard Rodgers
© Copyright 1938 (Renewed) by Chappell & Co.

Rights for the Extended Renewal Term in the U.S. Controlled by Williamson Music and WB Music Corp. o/b/o The Estate Of Lorenz Hart
This arrangement © Copyright 2018 by Williamson Music and WB Music Corp. o/b/o The Estate Of Lorenz Hart International Copyright Secured.
All Rights Reserved.
Reprinted by Permission of Hal Leonard LLC

"The Devil You Know" from *Side Show*
Words by Bill Russell
Music by Henry Krieger
© Copyright 1994 MIROKU MUSIC (ASCAP), 3 Sheridan Square, Apt. 15A, New York, NY 10014 and STILLBILL MUSIC
(ASCAP), 1500 Broadway, Suite 2001, New York, NY 10036
This arrangement © Copyright 2018 MIROKU MUSIC (ASCAP), 3 Sheridan Square, Apt. 15A, New York, NY 10014 and
STILLBILL MUSIC (ASCAP), 1500 Broadway, Suite 2001, New York, NY 10036
International Copyright Secured
All Rights Reserved
Reprinted by Permission of Hal Leonard LLC

"Far From The Home I Love" from *Fiddler on the Roof*
Words by Sheldon Harnick
Music by Jerry Bock
© Copyright 1964 Bock IP LLC and Mayerling Productions, Ltd.
Copyright Renewed 1992
This arrangement © Copyright 2018 Bock IP LLC and Mayerling Productions, Ltd.
All Rights for Mayerling Productions, Ltd. Administered by R&H Music, a Division of Rodgers & Hammerstein: an Imagem Company
International Copyright Secured
All Rights Reserved
Reprinted by Permission of Hal Leonard LLC

"Good Morning Baltimore" from *Hairspray*
Music by Marc Shaiman
Lyrics by Marc Shaiman and Scott Wittman
© Copyright 2000 Winding Brook Way Music and Walli Woo Entertainment
This arrangement © Copyright 2018 Winding Brook Way Music and Walli Woo Entertainment
All Rights Administered by Universal Music Corp.
All Rights Reserved
Used by Permission
Reprinted by Permission of Hal Leonard LLC

"Hello!" from *The Book Of Mormon*
Words and Music by Randolph Parker, Matthew Stone and Robert Lopez
© Copyright 2011 Furry Carlos Music Publishing Inc. and Only For Now, Inc.

This arrangement © Copyright 2018 Furry Carlos Music Publishing Inc. and Only For Now, Inc.
All Rights for Furry Carlos Music Publishing Inc. Administered by Kobalt Songs Music Publishing
All Rights Reserved
Used by Permission
Reprinted by Permission of Hal Leonard LLC

"I Will Prevail" from *Wonderland: A New Alice*
Music by Frank Wildhorn
Lyrics by Jack Murphy
© Copyright 2011 Bronx Flash Music, Inc. (ASCAP), Ryan Samuel Melodies (ASCAP) and Lily Bird Music (BMI) This arrangement © Copyright 2018 Bronx Flash Music, Inc. (ASCAP), Ryan Samuel Melodies (ASCAP) and Lily Bird
Music (BMI)
All Rights for the world Controlled and Administered by Bronx Flash Music, Inc. and Kenwon Music
International Copyright Secured. All Rights Reserved.
Reprinted by Permission of Hal Leonard LLC

"In The Beginning" from *Children of Eden*
Music and Lyrics by Stephen Schwartz
© Copyright 1989, 1998, 2000 Grey Dog Music (ASCAP)
This arrangement © Copyright 2018 Grey Dog Music (ASCAP)
Publishing and allied rights for "In The Beginning" Administered by Williamson Music, a Division of Hammerstein & Rodgers : an Imagem Company
International Copyright Secured.
All Rights Reserved.
www.stephenschwartz.com
Reprinted by Permission of Hal Leonard LLC

"It Only Takes A Moment" from *Hello, Dolly!*
Music and Lyric by Jerry Herman
© Copyright 1963 (Renewed) Jerry Herman
This arrangement © Copyright 2018 Jerry Herman
All Rights Controlled by Edwin H. Morris & Company, A Division of MPL Music Publishing, Inc.
All Rights Reserved.
Reprinted by Permission of Hal Leonard LLC.

"Man Of La Mancha (I, Don Quixote)" from *Man Of La Mancha*
Lyric by Joe Darion
Music by Mitch Leigh
© Copyright 1965 (Renewed 1994) Andrew Scott, Inc. and Helena Music Corp. This arrangement © Copyright 2018 Andrew Scott, Inc. and Helena Music Corp. International Copyright Secured.
All Rights Reserved.
Reprinted by Permission of Hal Leonard LLC.

"Maybe" from *Annie*
Lyric by Martin Charnin

Music by Charles Strouse
© Copyright 1977 (Renewed) Edwin H. Morris & Company, A Division of MPL Music Publishing, Inc. and Charles Strouse Publishing
This arrangement © Copyright 2018 Edwin H. Morris & Company, A Division of MPL Music Publishing, Inc. and Charles Strouse Publishing
All Rights for Charles Strouse Publishing Administered by WB Music Corp.
All Rights Reserved
Reprinted by Permission of Hal Leonard LLC

"My Favorite Things" from *The Sound of Music*
Lyrics by Oscar Hammerstein II
Music by Richard Rodgers
© Copyright 1959 by Richard Rodgers and Oscar Hammerstein II
Copyright Renewed
This arrangement © Copyright 2018 by Williamson Music, a Division of Rodgers & Hammerstein: an Imagem Company, owner of publication and allied rights throughout the world. International Copyright Secured.
All Rights Reserved.
Reprinted by Permission of Hal Leonard LLC

"On My Way" from *Violet*
Music by Jeanine Tesori
Lyrics by Brian Crawley
© Copyright 1997 That"s Music To My Ears and Bayfield Music
This arrangement © Copyright 2018 That"s Music To My Ears and Bayfield Music
All Rights Reserved
Used by Permission
Reprinted by Permission of Hal Leonard LLC

"Popular" from *Wicked*
Music and Lyrics by Stephen Schwartz
© Copyright 2003 Stephen Schwartz
This arrangement © Copyright 2018 Stephen Schwartz
All Rights Reserved
Used by Permission of Grey Dog Music (ASCAP)
Reprinted by Permission of Hal Leonard LLC

"Safer" from *First Date*
Music and Lyrics by Alan Zachary and Michael Weiner
Copyright © 2014 Alan Zachary and Michael Weiner
This arrangement Copyright © 2018 Alan Zachary and Michael Weiner
All Rights Administered Worldwide by Imagem Music, LLC
All Rights Reserved
Used by Permission
Reprinted by Permission of Hal Leonard LLC

"Santa Fe" from *Newsies*
Music by Alan Menken

Lyrics by Jack Feldman
© Copyright 1992, 2012 Wonderland Music Company, Inc. and Camp Songs Music
This arrangement © Copyright 2018 Wonderland Music Company, Inc. and Camp Songs Music
All Rights Administered by Wonderland Music Company, Inc.
All Rights Reserved.
Used by Permission. Reprinted by Permission of Hal Leonard LLC

"Seventy Six Trombones" from *The Music Man*
By Meredith Willson
© Copyright 1957 (Renewed) Frank Music Corp. and Meredith Willson Music
This arrangement © Copyright 2018 Frank Music Corp. and Meredith Willson Music
All Rights Reserved.
Reprinted by Permission of Hal Leonard LLC.

"Someday" from *The Wedding Singer*
Music by Matthew Sklar
Lyrics by Chad Beguelin
© Copyright 2006 Matthew Sklar Music (ASCAP) and Chad Beguelin Music (ASCAP)
This arrangement © Copyright 2018 Matthew Sklar Music (ASCAP) and Chad Beguelin Music (ASCAP)
Worldwide Rights for Matthew Sklar Music and Chad Beguelin Music Administered by Cherry Lane
Music Publishing Company, Inc.
International Copyright Secured.
All Rights Reserved.
Reprinted by Permission of Hal Leonard LLC.

"Someone Like You" from *Jekyll & Hyde*
Words and Music by Leslie Bricusse and Frank Wildhorn
© Copyright 1997 Painted Desert Music Corp. on behalf of Stage And Screen Music Inc., BMG Ruby
Songs,
Scaramanga Music, Inc. and Reservoir Media Music
This arrangement © Copyright 2018 Painted Desert Music Corp. on behalf of Stage And Screen Music Inc.,
BMG Ruby
Songs, Scaramanga Music, Inc. and Reservoir Media Music
All Rights for BMG Ruby Songs and Scaramanga Music, Inc. Administered by BMG Rights Management
(US) LLC All Rights for Reservoir Media Music Administered by Reservoir Media Management, Inc.
Reservoir Media Music Administered by Alfred Music
International Copyright Secured.
All Rights Reserved.
Used by Permission.
Reprinted by Permission of Hal Leonard LLC

"Still Hurting" from *The Last Five Years*
Music and Lyrics by Jason Robert Brown
© Copyright 2002 by Jason Robert Brown
This arrangement © Copyright 2018 by Jason Robert Brown
All Rights Controlled by Semolina Farfalle Music Co. Inc. (ASCAP)
International Copyright Secured.

All Rights Reserved.
Reprinted by Permission of Hal Leonard LLC

"Summer Nights" from *Grease*
Lyric and Music by Warren Casey and Jim Jacobs
© Copyright 1972 Warren Casey and Jim Jacobs
© Copyright Renewed 2000 Jim Jacobs and The Estate Of Warren Casey
This arrangement © Copyright Renewed 2018 Jim Jacobs and The Estate Of Warren Casey
All Rights Administered by Edwin H. Morris & Company, A Division of MPL Music Publishing, Inc.
All Rights Reserved
Reprinted by Permission of Hal Leonard LLC

"The Surrey With The Fringe On Top" from *Oklahoma!*
Lyrics by Oscar Hammerstein II
Music by Richard Rodgers
© Copyright 1943 by Williamson Music, a Division of Rodgers & Hammerstein: an Imagem Company.
Copyright Renewed
This arrangement © Copyright 2018 by Williamson Music, a Division of Rodgers & Hammerstein: an Imagem Company International Copyright Secured
All Rights Reserved
Reprinted by Permission of Hal Leonard LLC

"There"s No Business Like Show Business" from *Annie Get Your Gun*
Words and Music by Irving Berlin
© Copyright 1946 by Irving Berlin
Copyright Renewed
This arrangement © Copyright 2018 by the Estate of Irving Berlin
International Copyright Secured
All Rights Reserved
Reprinted by Permission of Hal Leonard LLC

"You"ll Never Walk Alone" from *Carousel*
Lyrics by Oscar Hammerstein II
Music by Richard Rodgers
© Copyright 1945 by Williamson Music, a Division of Rodgers & Hammerstein: an Imagem Company
Copyright Renewed
This arrangement © Copyright 2018 by Williamson Music, a Division of Rodgers & Hammerstein: an Imagem Company International Copyright Secured
All Rights Reserved
Reprinted by Permission of Hal Leonard LLC

"Come With me" from *The Boys from Syracuse*
By LORENZ HART and RICHARD RODGERS
Copyright© 1939 (Renewed) CHAPPELL & CO., INC. And WILLIAMSON MUSIC COMPANY
All Rights Reserved
Used By Permission of Alfred Music
50% Control In The United States 100% Control in the Rest of the World

"Maybe" from *Annie*
By Lorenz Hart and Richard Rodgers
Copyright© 1939 (Renewed) Chappell & Co., Inc. and Williamson Music Company
All Rights Reserved
Used By Permission of Alfred Music
50% Control in the World

"What Did I Have That I Don"t Have?" from *On a Clear Day You Can See Forever*
Lyrics by Alan Jay Lerner Music by Burton Lane
Copyright © 1965 (Renewed) by Alan Jay Lerner and Burton Lane Publication and Allied Right s Assigned to Chappell & Co., INC .
All Rights Reserved
Used By Permission of Alfred Music
100% Control in the World

"Somewhere Over the Rainbow" from *The Wizard of Oz*
Music by Harold Arlen Lyrics by E.Y. Harburg Copyright© 1938 (Renewed) Metro-Goldwyn-Mayer INC.
© 1939 (Renewed) Emi Feist Catalog Inc.
All Right s Controlled and Administered by Emi Feist Catalog In C. (Publishing) an d Alfred Music (Print)
All Rights Reserved
Used By Permission of Alfred Music
100% Control in the World - Excluding Europe

"Lucky to Be Me" from *On The Town*
Lyric s by Betty Comden and Adolph Green Music by Leonard Bernstein
Copyright © 1944 (Renewed) WB Music Corp.
All Right s Reserved
Used By Permission of Alfred Music
100% Control in the World

"Alone in the Universe" from *Seussica, the Musical*
Lyrics by Lynn Aherns Music by Stephen Flaherty
Copyright © 2001 WB Music Corp., Pen and Perseverance and Hillsdale Music, Inc.
All Rights Administered by WB Music Corp.
All Rights Reserved
Used By Permission of Alfred Music
100% Control in the World

"Treat Me Rough" from *Crazy Girl*
Music and Lyrics by George Gerschwin and Ira Gershwin Copyright© 1944 (Renewed) WB Music Corp.
All Rights Reserved
Used By Permission of Alfred Music
100% Control in the World

"Your Daddy"s Son" from *Ragtime*
Lyrics by Lynn Ahrens Music by Stephen Flaherty
Copyright © 1997 WB Music Corp., Pen and Perseverance and Hillsdale Music, Inc.

All Rights Administered by WB Music Corp.
All Rights Reserved
Used By Permission of Alfred Music
100% Control in the World

"Always Starting Over" from *If/Then*
Lyrics by Brian Yorkey Music by Tom Kitt
Copyright © 2014 Lonely Satellite Music (BMI) and Tom Kitt Music (BMI)
All Rights Administered by Warner Tamblane Publishing Corp. (BMI) All Rights Reserved
Used By Permission of Alfred Music
100% Control in the World

"Go To Sleep Slumber Deep" from *Babes in Toyland*
Words by Glen MacDonough Music by Victor Herbert
Copyright© 1903 (Renewed) Warner Bros. Inc. . All Rights Reserved
Used By Permission of Alfred Music
100% Control in the World
(Public Domain in the United States)

"Too Darn Hot" from *Kiss Me Kate*
Words and Music by Cole Porter Copyright © 1949 by Cole Porter
Copyright Renewed and Assigned to John F. Wharton, Trustee of the Cole Porter Musical and Literary
Property Trusts
Publication and allied rights assigned to Chappell & Co. Inc. .
All Rights Reserved
Used By Permission of Alfred Music

100% Control in the World

"Pulled" from *The Addams Family*
Words and Music by Andrew Lippa
© 2009 Lippa Songs
All Rights Administered by WB Music Corp. All Rights Reserved
Used By Permission of Alfred Music
For our 100% in the world

"As Long as He Needs Me" from *Oliver!*
Lyrics and Music by Lionel Bart
© Copyright 1960 (Renewed) Lakeview Music Co., Ltd., London, England
TRO-Hollis Music, Inc., New York, controls all publication rights for the USA and Canada
International Copyright Secured Made in U.S.A.
All Rights Reserved Including Public Performance For Profit

"Someone Like You" from *Jekyll and Hyde*
Lyrics by Leslie Bricusse Music by Frank Wildhorn
© 1990, 1995 Reservoir Media Music (ASCAP), BMG Gold Songs, BMG Ruby Songs, LES Etoiles de la
Musique and Stage and Screen Music Ltd. .

All Rights for Reservoir Media Music (ASCAP) Administered by Reservoir Media Management, Inc.
Reservoir Media Music (ASCAP) Administered by Alfred Music.
All Rights Reserved
Used By Permission of Alfred Music

"I Got Rhythm" from *Girl Crazy*
Music and Lyrics by George Gerschwin and Ira Gershwin
© 1930 (Renewed) WB Music Corp. and Ira Gershwin Music
All Rights Administered by WB Music Corp.
By Permission of Alfred Music
For our 100% in USA and Canada

"Comedy Tonight" from *A Funny Thing Happened on the Way to the Forum*
All Rights Administered by Chappell & Co., Inc.
© 1962 (Renewed) Burthen Music Company, Inc.
Music and Lyrics by Stephen Sondheim
By Permission of Alfred Music
For our 100% in USA and Canada

"Time Stops" from *Big Fish*
All Rights Reserved
Words and Music by Andrew Lippa
© 2013 Lippa Songs.
All Rights Administered by WB Music Corp.
By Permission of Alfred Music
For our 100% in USA and Canada

"Leavin"s Not The Only Way To Go" from *Big River*
Words Copyright and © Music 1985 by Sony/Roger ATV Miller Songs LLC and Roger Miller Music.
All This Rights Arrangement by Administered Copyright © Sony/ 2018 ATV Sony/Music ATV Publishing,
LLC 424 and Church Roger Street, Miller Suite Music. I 200,
Nashville, TN 37219
International Copyright Secured All Rights Reserved
Reprinted by Permission of Hal Leonard LLC

"Happy To Keep His Dinner Warm" from *How to Succeed in Business Without Really Trying*
By Frank Laesser
© This arrangement 1961 (Renewed) © 2018 Frank Music Corp.
All Rights Reserved
Reprinted by Permission of Hal Leonard LLC

INDEX

CPSIA information can be obtained
at www.ICGtesting.com
Printed in the USA
LVHW022233110723
752230LV00032B/955

9 781350 001756